You and AT *

* AUTOGENIC TRAINING—
THE REVOLUTIONARY WAY
TO RELAXATION
AND INNER PEACE

You and AT*

* AUTOGENIC TRAINING—

THE REVOLUTIONARY WAY

TO RELAXATION

AND INNER PEACE

Karl Robert Rosa

TRANSLATED FROM THE GERMAN BY
HELEN TUSCHLING

SATURDAY REVIEW PRESS | E. P. DUTTON & CO., INC.

NEW YORK

ISBN: 0-8415-0407-5

Library of Congress Cataloging in Publication Data

Rosa, Karl Robert, 1921–
  You and AT

  Translation of Das ist autogenes Training.
  Bibliography: p.
  1. Autogenic training. I. Title.
RC499.A8R6713 1973   616.8'916'2   75-28290

To the memory of my teacher
Professor J. H. Schultz

CONTENTS

ABOUT THIS BOOK

What is autogenic training? Autogenic training is an exact, clearly defined method of self-hypnosis, and the means to a new, relaxed enjoyment of one's physical existence.

The purpose of this book is to inform you about autogenic training. More and more doctors are advising patients who suffer from functional disorders to take up autogenic training. In those cases where previous checkups have revealed a functional disorder but no organic illness, this has proven to be excellent advice.

The AT (autogenic training) method is well established. Dr. Johannes H. Schultz, the father of the method, wrote a comprehensive instruction manual which is indispensable to all those teaching or learning to teach the method, but until now there has been no book designed for the person who wishes to approach AT on his own with the aim of expanding his self-awareness and increasing his sense of well-being. *You and AT* presents the original AT method clearly and without distortion. The author of this book, himself one of

Schultz's pupils, can speak from decades of experience with AT in his native Germany. The results of his work, presented here, summarize the insights he has gained as an instructor and in individual case work with people who have learned, through AT, to experience and to accept themselves.

It is difficult to learn AT reliably all by oneself. But anyone who is prepared to master the technique with the help of an instructor will never regret it. AT is a tested therapeutic method which is by no means intended only for those who are seriously disturbed or ill. AT, properly learned and regularly practiced, makes a person who already feels well feel much better.

This book is an invitation to the reader to become an AT trainee.

INTRODUCTION

Find Thyself a Teacher!
(Pirke Aboth—Sayings of the Fathers, 1:6)

The importance of the instructor in AT has been recognized ever since J. H. Schultz's original presentation of the method. My concern, in this book, is with the positive content of the relationship between the instructor and the trainee, and my intention is primarily to anticipate and to answer specific questions about AT, to awaken interest in the method, and to indicate some of its possible applications.

An intensive course in AT must be seen as an exchange of thoughts and experiences between the instructor and the trainee. During the period of instruction, this discrepancy of experience gradually diminishes: instructor and trainee finally come to exchange thoughts and experiences as equals.

In addition to this combination of methodical instruction and personal exchange, it is my suggestion—and experience confirms its value—that the trainee make detailed notes of his perceptions while practicing and bring these to each session. The trainee thus has the details with which to enrich his talks with his instructor, who can then help him to interpret the notes and to understand the results of his exercises. These notes, which should not be too elaborate—merely a brief record of the essentials—reinforce the instruction and encourage the trainee to play an active role in the session, thus insuring a genuine dialogue.

Like every learnable technique, AT has its own fundamental rules which cannot be disregarded without jeopardizing its success.

One of the most fundamental rules is frequent and regular repetition. For this reason, it has been customary ever since the 1920s to recommend two brief practice sessions a day. As we know from the findings of research into the psychology of learning, two short sessions at different times of the day are vastly preferable to one lengthy session, and certainly to any sort of determined marathon training. Frequent repetition of material or experience is more conducive to retention than a time-consuming prolonged struggle with a large amount of material.

A second fundamental rule of learning AT is the thorough assimilation of what has already been learned before proceeding further: before going on to each new step, the previous steps must always be repeated. For example, when learning the fourth standard exercise, the trainee must go through the mood formula and standard exercises one, two, and three before he adds the new material. This must be done in every practice session. The new material can then occupy the bulk of the practice time at that particular session.

Assigning the individual practice sessions to regular times of the day, and if possible linking them with other regularly recurring actions, allows the trainee to create a pattern which aids the learning process and which also forms a permanent bond between the material learned and other thoughts and actions unconnected with it.

Before attempting to explain what AT is and what it offers, here is a very brief sketch of AT as a whole, as it was presented in Dr. Schultz's original training pamphlet.

The basic stage of AT consists of a series of standard exercises, which could also be called "orientations," and a preliminary formula—called the "mood formula"—which can be seen as a sort of motto for the whole of AT. In its simplest form, this is the structure of AT, step by step:

A. The mood formula: "I am at peace."
B. The six basic exercises:
1. "Right arm [or, for left-handed people, the left arm] very heavy."
2. "Right [or left] hand warm."
3. "Pulse calm and strong."
4. "Breath calm and regular."
5. "Solar plexus glowing warm."
6. "Forehead pleasantly cool."

Anyone taking part in an AT course will soon realize that these formulations may be varied to some extent. An experienced teacher can also change the sequence of the formulae at his discretion, usually depending on the health and the symptoms of the trainee. This is the teacher's responsibility, and his alone. The trainee should not tie himself to the phrases given here or in an exercise pamphlet; he should use those phrases which his instructor has used with him, and always in exactly the same sequence.

FOREWORD

by A. S. Paterson, M.D.

Many doctors and members of the public in Britain, Canada, and the United States will welcome Helen Tuschling's translation of Dr. Rosa's book about autogenic training. AT has long been the most widely used and popular treatment for functional nervous diseases in Germany, as well as being employed as a peace-inducing method of total relaxation. I would like to explain briefly how AT is related to hypnosis and autohypnosis, the nature of which is better understood in the English-speaking world than the more specialized techniques of AT.

Hypnosis is a modification of consciousness. Other modifications are dreamless sleep, dream sleep, daydreaming and, in the other direction, alert concentration. One characteristic of hypnosis is that the individual's field of consciousness is restricted, often to the extent of blocking all incoming sensations except the voice of the hypnotist. The hypnotized person may mistake the images created in his mind by the hypnotist's voice for images coming from the real world. Thus, a stage hypnotist might hand a member of the audience a poker and tongs and say that the pair of tongs was a violin and the poker, a bow, and the audience would laugh to see the victim try to play the violin. But hypnotism, used therapeutically rather than for entertainment, can be a powerful mode of influencing people's behavior and health.

Since AT employs a form of hypnosis induced by the trainee himself, it is important to understand the effect of hypnosis on the autonomic nervous system (ANS) which supplies the internal organs of the body. First of all, the nervous system is divided into two parts, the central nervous system, which is under the control of the will, and which influences the contractions and tone of the voluntary muscles; and the autonomic nervous system, which is not under the control of the will. Its branches supply various organs of the body such as the heart, stomach, and liver, but cannot make a person's heart beat faster or slower at will. The ANS, in its turn, is also divided into two parts. The mainly sympathetic system comes into action when a person is working hard, and, even more strongly, when he is in danger. The other system, the parasympathetic system, comes into play when a person is feeling secure and relaxed and wants to build up strength through repose. Its action is generally accompanied by a feeling of well-being.

The changes which occur during the dominance of the sympathetic system enable us to meet danger more successfully; the changes are those which we associate with fear: we tremble with fear because our muscles must be tense to be ready for a fight, or for flight. The heart races with fear to pump oxygen and sugar to the muscles. Vision and hearing become more acute. The breathing becomes quicker, to get as much oxygen into the blood as possible. The three reservoirs of the body may be emptied, to enable us to move faster.

Primitive man experienced a rhythm in his life in which the danger reaction alternated with the security reaction so that, once back in a safe place, he could rest, sleep, eat and relax. ANS is important in relation to the hypnotic state. It is closely associated with the successful reaction to extreme stress, and is therefore of particular importance to athletes. And the student of AT who "switches over" to the "hypnoid" or hypnotic state that occurs in AT is now in the calm, pleasant, relaxed state which is characteristic of the parasympathetic or security reaction. In many cases, the individual, before treatment, had been in a tense, anxious state and so he welcomes the change to a condition of calm. This is the state also in which the trainee changes from directing his attention outward to his material surroundings, and turns his attention inward to his subjective experiences, often of a dreamlike nature, in which he sees various colors and shapes. This experience occurs more in the advanced stage of AT. At this point, the trainee may have strange or mystical experiences in which he sometimes feels that he is floating.

Scientific investigation has shown further that in the hypnotic state there is some degree of blocking sensory input from the environment. For this reason, the individual can experience hallucinations and other dreamlike symptoms that are characteristic of so-called "sensory deprivation." This occurs either in patients who have to lie motionless for a period of time in solitary surroundings, or in persons, such as Arctic explorers, who must remain in perpetual darkness, silence, and solitude. It is also, of course, the condition of an astronaut. In the case of an AT trainee, however, the condition is beneficial, for the therapist finds the analysis of his thoughts in this dreamlike state possibly easier to interpret and more revealing than the Freudian analysis of dreams.

The most significant benefit, however, which the trainee acquires from being in the hypnotic state is that he gradually gains some measure of control over his autonomic functions. Doctors, recognizing this, now have more confidence in employing hypnosis, whether according to the tenets of AT, or otherwise. Disorders of the digestive system, such as loss of appetite or its opposite, nibbling between meals, are among the types of malfunction of the nervous system which have been successfully treated. Irregular beating of the heart and high blood pressure have also responded to hypnosis. Asthma and migraine are two other common complaints that have been the object of recent hypnosis research, and hypnosis is now commonly used as an adjunct in the treatment of stammer. Alcoholism and drug abuse can also be treated by hypnosis. As hypnosis inhibits incoming sensations, it is successful in many cases in either totally inhibiting pain while the individual is in a trancelike state, or accelerating the natural tendency, in a calm individual, for any pain to be finally inhibited. A world congress on pain, held at Rottach-Egern in Bavaria in 1969, concluded that conservative psychological treatment including some form of hypnosis should always be carried out, if possible, surgery is considered.[1]

There are two main groups of people who are motivated to

1. J. P. Payne and R. A. P. Burt, eds., *Pain* (London: Churchill Livingstone, 1972).

embark on an AT course. Some people turn to AT because of some functional disorder or because of some floating anxiety, while others are interested in psychology and a deeper understanding of the workings of the human mind, or simply in increased relaxation and well-being. Interested students of AT are not put off by the necessity for constant repetition of formulae, because the exercises take a shorter and shorter period of time as the trainee masters them.

AT consists of the basic training, which is a complete course in itself, and an advanced course which is undertaken only by a much smaller number of trainees. Its study is limited to those who have mastered the basic course. In this advanced treatment, induction of the desired state is brought about by the ocular fixation method, whereby the trainee gazes at an object a few feet from his eyes. There is a similarity between the hypnoidal state and that of dream sleep, so that the therapist can employ psychoanalytic techniques to probe the trainee's deeper motivations. Here, the student may undergo experiences of a religious and mystical character, some of which may reveal aspects of his personality of which he was not previously aware.

One remarkable result of the advanced course is the ability of the trainee to endure great stress and danger, to experience a total loss of the sense of his own individuality, and to feel one with a part of the universe, an experience which is often described by practitioners of some types of Oriental meditation. Dr. Hannes Lindemann has written about his own experiences in crossing the Atlantic alone in an open boat, a venture which he believed would have ended in failure if he had not previously subjected himself to an extremely rigorous course of AT. When under great stress he experienced symptoms similar to those described by some Oriental meditators: he temporarily lost his sense of personal identity and felt a sort of mystical union with a part of nature—the ocean.[2]

The World Psychiatric Association Congress at Montreal in 1961 included a section devoted to the discussion of AT. It was led by Dr. W. Luthe who has written several volumes on autogenic training in collaboration with Professor J. H. Schultz. Dr. Luthe has taught and practiced AT for many years in Montreal. Dr. D. Langen, now Professor at Mainz in West Germany, who has written widely in favor of AT, gave a description of a modification of AT called graduated active hypnosis (GAH) which can take less time and is, in his opinion, more suitable for some types of cases. Dr. Rosa once remarked that Dr. Schultz had the greatest difficulty in retaining his celebrated composure when a junior colleague suggested modification of AT. This was chiefly because uniformity of technique made it easier to plan experiments and clinical trials and thereby to add to scientific knowledge. However, both Schultz and Dr. Rosa have paid generous tributes to the good results obtained by similar methods, even though they themselves strongly preferred the orthodox AT. They maintain that AT is a science and not a cult, and have been known to employ strong words against those who "betrayed the cause."

Throughout history the chief aim of psychologists has been to enable men to control irrational impulses that can lead to dangerous aggression. In Switzerland and in Germany there

---

2. H. Lindemann, M.D., *Relieve Tension the Autogenic Way* (New York: Peter H. Wyden, Inc., 1973).

has been a succession of three extremely gifted doctors who have recognized that the "hypnoidal" state enables an individual to gain control not only over his body but also over his emotions. The first and second to recognize this were world famous experts in the anatomy of the brain and the nervous system, and the most recent, Dr. Schultz, was also a neurologist who at one time worked in the same hospital as Hans Berger, who discovered brain waves and the science of electroencephalography. Schultz no doubt was inspired to some extent by Dr. Berger.

The first of the three men who contributed to the creation of AT was August Forel (1845–1931) who was Professor of Psychiatry at Zurich. He was primarily preoccupied with the structure of the brain and was joint discoverer of the neuron (nerve cell) which is the unit of the brain and nervous system. He also wrote a text book on hypnosis in 1889 which went into twelve editions. He taught both hypnosis and the pathology of the brain to a young genius called Oskar Vogt, who later became the chief European expert on the brain. He discovered the method of inducing a hypnotic state by having the patient concentrate on heaviness and warmth. This finding was greatly developed by J. H. Schultz who elaborated the system of AT on the basis of Vogt's work.

Schultz tried to obtain the benefits of age-old practices of Oriental yoga and meditation while interpreting their phenomena in the light of Western science. It is a measure of his success that a number of Indian psychiatrists are now practicing AT in preference to yoga or meditation.

Another field where AT has made its influence felt is in space travel. Could astronauts train themselves to pass into a state of autohypnosis for a fairly prolonged period? If the astronaut could pass into a state of controlled catalepsy, he could lower his basic metabolic rate to a minimum, and could thus obtain extended benefits from his food and oxygen supply. In this state, he could inhibit hunger, thirst, pain and discomfort and, at least for a time, distress from heat or cold. He could retain the contents of his bladder and bowels for longer periods also. It is of interest that Dr. Klaus Thomas, a pupil and close friend of the late Dr. Schultz, came to the United States to visit the National Aeronautics and Space Administration in 1972 to discuss such uses of AT. Schultz would have been proud of the remarkable enthusiasm shown by so many of his pupils, such as Dr. Rosa, who have carried on his work.

One incident in the life of Professor Schultz that will always remain in my memory occurred at the World Congress of Psychiatry in Madrid in 1966 when several young psychiatrists read promising papers on AT. "Ah," he said, "I have lived to listen to an account of the work of my spiritual grandchildren!"

You and AT *

* AUTOGENIC TRAINING—
THE REVOLUTIONARY WAY
TO RELAXATION
AND INNER PEACE

I

AUTOGENIC TRAINING —
WHAT IS IT?

How autogenic training was developed

"AT was developed in direct connection with experiences of hypnosis." With this unambiguous statement in 1929, J. H. Schultz clearly indicated the derivation and nature of AT. The source of the technique in hypnosis can be shown only against a coherent picture of hypnosis itself.

Medical hypnosis is not a new technique; it can be traced back to antiquity. Mesmer is a more recent innovator in suggestive hypnotic treatment, although his "magnetism" is not purely hypnotic technique as it is understood today. Toward the end of the nineteenth century, Braid used hypnotic techniques based on theories which are still valid today. Of greater importance was the work of the French school of Nancy, with which Freud had close connections. By the turn of the century, the technique of hypnosis was already extremely well developed. One of the leading figures in this field was Oskar Vogt, the teacher of J. H. Schultz. In the first decade of this century, Schultz adopted Vogt's technique of fractionated hypnosis and developed and refined it further.

Medical hypnosis is essentially a method of putting a person to sleep; the patient, lying outstretched, is brought to a state of total physical relaxation and immobility. The various means of inducing sleep are themselves of roughly equal merit. The patient does not really fall into a sleeping state, but rather into a drowsiness with diminished consciousness of the external world and the greatest possible apathy. With the help of verbal suggestions which encourage a state of pleasant, untroubled relaxation, the patient becomes completely passive at the commencement of the hypnotic state. His concentration is focused on the hypnotist and his words, and his interest gradually turns to an exclusive concentration on those inner experiences which the hypnotist has conjured up for him. It must be stressed that a properly hypnotized person is not reduced to a passive, will-less subject. His passivity means a relinquishing of spontaneous, self-directed activity in favor of an ability to experience and an openness toward experience the content and quality of which are indicated by the hypnotist. In this state of passive self-experiencing, the patient enjoys the beneficial effect of complete muscular relaxation and a regulating of the sympathetic nervous system. With this inner experience as a foundation, he is able to risk confrontation with traumatic events from his past life or with present conflicts. With the help of the hypnotist, who guides him and who provides this vivid density of experience, psychological transferences and resolutions can come about. Here lies the real therapeutic nature of this treatment.

Like the beginning, the end of every hypnotic session follows a prescribed pattern. This guarantees a process that is free of any disturbing side or after effects. Of course, such a technique must be learned and thoroughly mastered by every hypnotist. An amateur playing around with this process could cause uncontrollable havoc with serious aftereffects in the organism of the patient.

Medical hypnosis, like all medical treatment, has its indications, i.e. symptoms which call for its use. Hypnosis is indicated for certain immediate psychic conflicts that are of the nature of a spiritual trauma. It is also indicated for long-term psycho-physiological illnesses and maladjustments the origins of which are either obscure or no longer remembered. Hypnosis can reveal the causal connections and, by consciously re-creating the forgotten conflict and intensive working with it, can bring about a cure. Where it is indicated, hypnosis has had excellent success as a treatment with no negative side effects. The only disadvantage of hypnosis is the prolonged dependence of the patient on the hypnotist, at least during the period of treatment.

At the turn of the century, attempts were already being made to release the hypnosis patient from this frequently bothersome dependence and put him on his own feet—to prescribe a hypnosis which he could carry on by himself after an initial course of treatment. The question was whether or not a methodical and reliable self-hypnosis was feasible. If it was, what were its technical possibilities and what its limitations?

The techniques of hypnosis cannot be used in self-hypnosis as they stand. The entry into and the return from the hypnotic state—in heterohypnosis a matter of the consummate technical mastery of the hypnotist—had to be modified for autonomous attempts. In the early days of research into auto-hypnosis, the young J. H. Schultz was working as a hospital doctor, and was much more thorough than several others who researched and published in this field during the first two decades of this century. He made an intensive study of the psychological processes involved in learning, and also of the physiological basis of bodily changes under hypnosis. The result of this comprehensive research was autogenic training, unquestionably the best method of autohypnotic exercises—and, moreover, harmless, provided the trainee learns the method exactly and masters it in depth through continuous practice.

The method of autogenic training

The goal of an AT session is a hypnotic state of light trance. In this respect, AT must be considered as an autohypnotic method. Various other available techniques, no matter how successful they might be in some cases, are based on a relaxation of the organism which need not show any sign of a trancelike state. The trance, a state of shallow hypnosis, is characterized by the seeking, attaining, and remaining in an experiential level of diminished consciousness. It follows that, with the lowering of consciousness, all the organic processes, including self-awareness, take place on a different level than when the person is fully conscious or asleep.

The diminished consciousness of the trancelike state gives the subject the experiential field necessary to reach the goal of each exercise, as well as the specific quality of experience at this level of consciousness and the specific mode of relaxation. This latter is not to be confused with sleeplike drowsiness or vacant dozing. It is the particular attentiveness to the physical processes involved and to the emotional content that accompanies them which gives the light trance its unmistakable quality.

The physical signs of the trance are as follows: the skeletal muscles, the "antagonistic pairs" as they are called, are relaxed. We speak of a loss of "tone," and by this we mean the reduction of the permanent muscular tension that is essential for an active organism. The blood vessels, particularly in the extremities, are dilated and carry more blood. The blood is more evenly distributed throughout the body; this is subjectively perceived as a pleasant feeling of warmth. The rhythmical biological activities—respiration and heartbeat—find their own unforced pace and work at a reduced intensity but with optimum efficiency. This is experienced subjectively as pleasantly restful and harmonious. The whole abdominal cavity, as a result of this physical relaxation, functions smoothly and spontaneously. Subjectively, this has the surprising effect of drawing our attention to areas of the body of which we are generally unaware, and gives rise to a feeling of pleasant well-being.

The head does not participate in these physiological adjustments. Schultz coined the phrase "a cool, deconcentrated head." The experience as a whole is not a "mindless" one; however, those activities of the brain which are manifested in thinking and imagining are reduced, if not eliminated. In the place of concentrated thought there is a calm observation of the body's own self-awareness. Spontaneous ideas vanish. The subject, in the AT state, is aware of himself in all his senses but does not reflect on himself. The will as a complex activity of the personality is not eliminated, but rather is optimally concerned with attaining and retaining this pleasant state of being. And it is the will that both sets the goal and gives the impulse for the return from the AT state. The well-devised technique for the return allows the subject to decide of his own free will to take the necessary steps to end the session in spite of its pleasantness.

AT is the first viable alternative to those popular and invariably useless attempts to overcome states of physical or psychological malaise through "self-control" or similar intense expenditure of will power. Control is not the way to overcome a deficiency or to put the brakes on exaggerated, misdirected activity. The essential feature of self-determination through AT is that the free will of the subject has sufficient room to extend the limits and improve the quality of its psycho-physiological capabilities. One indication of the effectiveness of AT is that better athletic performances can be achieved by using AT than by determined, intensive physical training.

AT, which is still unsurpassed, is the oldest method to use the healing powers of a shallow trance that is induced frequently, daily, and independent of external circumstances. One who has mastered AT has a means of self-discovery which is unrivaled for coping both with illness and with ordinary daily life.

Yoga is often cited as a comparable or even superior technique, but yoga differs from AT both in basic questions of method and in concrete details. One important difference is that the two methods have arisen in totally different cultures with widely divergent aims. A more detailed comparison of the two methods can be found in the last chapter.

In the early years following the original publication of AT, doctors already familiar with the method, impressed by the universal experience of beneficial relaxation and the experiences of weight and warmth, raised a plea that as many people as possible should be made acquainted with AT. Schultz conducted his first series of comprehensive experiments in a Berlin school. Almost everyone with the interest and perseverance to learn AT was soon able to report positive results; when this became known, the use of AT quickly spread, and the trend has not yet been reversed. Adult-education establishments, rest homes, sanatoria, and similar institutions in Germany and elsewhere offer introductory courses in AT, leading interested people to work on it further themselves. In many places in Germany, Switzerland, Austria, and other Western countries, doctors and psychologists who have mastered the technique are engaged in teaching it, mainly to groups. Recently, AT has been recognized and practiced extensively in North and Central America as well as in Europe and in Russia, and its widespread acceptance and popularity everywhere are increasing.

There are a number of well-defined medical indications for the use of AT. And we also know of a few contraindications that suggest that it would be inadvisable to use AT. Finally, there is one serious condition which totally precludes the use of AT, namely acute psychotic states; and there are also limitations to the use of AT in the case of a few serious illnesses. But apart from this, most people are able to learn AT and, whether or not they are ill in any way, they can with the help of AT permanently influence their various psycho-physical states and bring them into harmony.

Any instruction in AT must take many facts into account; it is not possible to prescribe a uniform teaching method for all. The teacher must consider the size and composition of the group as well as the needs and expectations of those who wish to learn AT. In a general course, the instructor can briefly explain the nature of the method and then introduce the trainees at once to their own first experiences of AT. Obviously it would be outside the scope of such a course to expound the method in great detail and thus overburden the participants with too much information. So for a general introductory course—such as an adult-education class—it is sufficient and to the purpose if the course members are presented with the essentials in capsule form and then given the opportunity to experience the relaxation and to feel the experiences of weight and warmth.

Group instruction profits from the well-known group law of mutual intensification—each participant is stimulated and confirmed by the reports of the others. One common hazard, however, must be reduced or eliminated: in every group there are individuals who are timid and skeptical of their abilities, who all too easily experience failure. An AT instructor must be aware of this and from the very beginning try to keep these usually very keen and cooperative group members from giving in to the sense of failure. We can presuppose that an AT instructor who is working with groups has some knowledge of group theory. Although the instruction consists primarily of communicating facts, every learning group is also functioning as a group; this is just as true of an AT group as it is of any other. A member who is lagging behind the group in the results of his efforts must be given support, and the achievements which he himself doubts must be confirmed to him if he is not to drop out of the group completely.

How AT is taught

Pressure to achieve and effort to achieve play an important role in both individual and group instruction. One of the specific aims of AT is that trainees should free themselves as far as possible from all concepts of achievement. The danger of falling into the usual comparisons is, of course, greater in a group than in individual instruction. Shielding the trainee from a drive to achieve—his own or an external one—is more difficult in a large introductory course than in a small homogeneous group. This problem hardly arises in individual instruction.

An AT course in a sanatorium will, of course, be centered on the main illness of the inmates and on the key symptoms which AT is used to treat. Obviously such a course will be quite different from one in an institute for adult education; it can go even further in omitting theory and proceed directly to the pathological problem as its starting point. And in a sanatorium course, that step in the sequence of standard exercises most relevant to the treatment of the illness must be deferred till the end of the sequence. It is necessary to mention these variations because it sometimes happens that a person who has had an AT course in a sanatorium then joins another course on his release and becomes confused at the difference. The instructors in both courses can deal with such justifiable modifications, either in anticipation or retrospectively.

What is true of sanatorium groups is also relevant to groups in hospitals. As an AT instructor of groups or individuals in a hospital, I would point out to the patients, before their departure, the need for further AT and also the form in which it should be pursued.

One delicate question must be raised about instruction. No matter how far the method has been reduced to a clear step-by-step procedure, it is unavoidable that each instructor will teach AT in his own personal style. If a person who has begun learning AT transfers to another teacher, then that teacher should find out in detail how the AT has previously been done. This is not simply a matter of the solidarity among colleagues which would forbid one to call another's methods in question, but of insight into the variability of the process which can beneficially assimilate many special instructions and aids. Only when the second teacher knows clearly what has previously been taught can he use those foundations to help the trainee. It is not enough for a trainee to report laconically that he has already learned AT; if he does not know the new teacher needs more information, then the teacher must question him as far as is necessary. Too many instructors still ignore the need for a case history. If the trainee kept notes in the first course, the notes should be continued, even if note-keeping is not part of the present instructor's usual method. On the other hand, the new teacher, if he is continuing the instruction begun by another, can ask the trainee to begin keeping notes without in any way discrediting this absence from the first course.

Individual instruction in AT offers possibilities that cannot be exploited in any group, especially a large one. Individual instruction allows matters to be discussed casually and informally, and this can give an experienced teacher insight into the personality structure of the trainee. How much use he makes of this in the instruction or therapy depends on the sort of treatment his discretion indicates.

No instruction should fail to impress the trainee with the need for continuity of work on AT. A simple comparison makes this clearer than the lengthy explanation: Just as cycling or swimming are abilities of a psycho-physiological nature, which can be maintained only through continuous effort and which must be kept up by practice, so too is AT a psycho-physiological ability to experience and to structure one's experience. A course that is limited to a stay in a sanatorium and learned as a way of passing the time must remain fragmentary. It often happens that people, in the course of other treatment, tell their doctors that they once practiced AT. Such a report indicates that the person in question only picked up a smattering of AT and was thus not really able to make use of it.

How AT is practiced

A person beginning AT should be told at the outset that the basic premise of AT is that he practice it on his own. "Autogenic" refers here not only to the particular effectiveness of AT in distinction to heterohypnosis; the acquisition of the method is autogenic too. The AT instructor can only indicate the framework, pass on the necessary tools, and direct the course, guiding, correcting, helping. Mastering the method to the point of virtuosity is the result of continual, persistent, and patient work by the trainee himself.

The AT trainee must realize from the outset that it is *he* who acquires the method and develops it until it is *his* training. Of course, he does not develop his own method, but adopts a method for his own private use; he interiorizes the experience that he gains, deepens it by persistent detailed work, and brings everything into a firm relationship with his personality as a whole. Each trainee soon develops his own emphases which distinguish him from others using the same method. Any one of the six standard exercises can become the main focus of someone's training; everyone has his own favorite formula.

While learning, and certainly later while practicing, the trainee notices that one exercise succeeds for him better than another. Depending on the strength of his achievement drive, this might perhaps irritate him at first and lead him to conclude that he has failed or not done well enough with the other exercises. This subjective judgment can be quite wrong objectively. It is the duty of the instructor to give support and explanations, and the trainee should mention such experiences and reactions at once so that they can be discussed. Trying to hide such difficulties in the hope of "muddling through" can result only in impeding the further learning process.

The trainee's realization that he is doing something of great personal relevance needs to be tactfully supported by the instructor, who should draw the trainee's attention to this at every possible opportunity. Accommodating oneself to the learning process so that the daily short practice sessions have their secure place in one's everyday routine is of tremendous importance for the success of the course and for fruitful further work on AT over the years.

This firm place in one's outward life must correspond to an "inner place" within the trainee: a genuine, unforced willingness to proceed further and a desire for the customary training time, twice a day or more frequently. These are the unmistakable signs of that inner readiness which must accompany the conscious decision.

Above all, the trainee must be willing to let it happen. What is "it"? Each of the standard formulae of the basic course is like a friendly invitation to an organism that is prepared to relax. It should be understood that any "must," any command, even an indirect imperative, constitutes a bar to complete relaxation. To every phrase can be added the extended notion that allows for the unexpected: if, to start with, the formula reads "I am completely relaxed," then the added anticipation could be phrased as "If I imagine that I am completely relaxed, what happens then?" and the trainee, self-absorbed in contemplation, expecting relaxation, finds both relaxation and tension, distinct from each other, alternating with each other; he experiences the coming of peace gradually. If he does not demand an abrupt change, but simply allows whatever will happen to happen, then, in the course of a few minutes, he can experience a gradual relaxation, a transition from nonrest, even in particular parts of the body, to rest. It comes, not because it was forced, but because he could wait until it came.

Not a few trainees feel they have to conceal their training from their families or other people, just as some people are

embarrassed to admit that they are in analysis or on a diet. In
such cases, it seems to me, the right basic attitude has not
been established at the outset. AT done on the sly cannot
succeed in the end. The trainee must stand by his training.
Negative judgments about the method are rooted in igno-
rance, as we are not dealing here with some untested, faddish
novelty. No AT trainee need let himself be confused by anyone's remarks—not even by that professor of psychiatry,
himself a psychotherapist, who is said to have claimed that
AT is a matter for the massage parlors. I myself have often
had a patient tell me his family doctor had scornfully or skeptically asked, "What, you're doing AT with so-and-so?
Don't tell me you believe that nonsense!" In my courses we
do not polemicize against the ignorant, we just get on with
the work. Would that others followed this example!

Demythologizing AT

This heading leads one to expect that there is some myth or
other connected with AT, vague ideas about just what AT is,
what it can achieve, and the nature of the highest expectations that can be demanded of it.

There are two main aspects of the mythologizing of AT.
One is connected with the medical profession, the other with
the general public. In spite of many publications in medical
journals and in complete disregard of the effectiveness of
courses held regularly all over the Western world, most doctors still choose to ignore this tried and tested therapy. It took
a long time before AT was recognized as a treatment by the
German Ministry of Health, and there is still no general acceptance of AT as a specifically medical treatment. A birth, a

transfusion, putting a splint on a broken bone, pulling a tooth are generally understood to be medical services. Why is this not the case with AT?

Is AT some sort of hocus-pocus? Some doctors seem to regard it as such. Others treat the method uncritically as merely a sort of relaxation exercise which they mistakenly group with physiotherapy, and they pay no further attention to it.

Owing to the particular qualifications of its founder and his first students, AT was for a long time the reserve of neurologists and specialists in internal medicine. Then, many general practitioners followed, and gynecologists began to take a keen interest in it; it has still, however, not been integrated into general medical practice. Most medical schools still have no firm place for it in their curricula.

The mythologizing of AT among the general public usually derives from that favorite topic of conversation, one's health. A person who has had some experience with AT may meet another person who, though ill or dissatisfied with the results of conventional therapy, has never heard of it. Oral tradition, that eternal source of the wildest myths, arouses great expectations in the ignorant. One person hears another mention positive results. Will AT be able to help him, too, with his particular ailment? Immediately, he fears he will not be able to live up to the demands AT makes. But his need for help is stronger. The conversation usually ends with his taking down a name and address.

There are, alas, all too few critical people who, after their first accidental bit of information, actually take the initiative and seek out an AT instructor. Everywhere there are institutes, individuals, etc., who offer various sorts of "total relaxation'' or similar techniques, but if you are determined to find a genuine AT instructor, you will be able to do so. Perhaps the following resumé of the method will help you in your search.

AT, as developed by Prof. J. H. Schultz in Germany, is a clearly structured and purposefully used method of self-hypnosis. It derives from medical hypnosis. It should, strictly speaking, be taught only by a doctor, and every course of instruction should be preceded by a physical checkup. AT is a distinctive treatment involving the organic processes of the body, malfunctions of which can be alleviated by bringing the regulative functions (sympathetic and parasympathetic) into harmony. This adjustment, together with a general relaxation and improved economy of function, is achieved by psycho-pedagogic means. Autosuggestion brings about a shallow trance with diminished consciousness and a turning of the attention inwards. Structure, attainment, and further development are grounded in the general truths of the psychology of learning. The instructor plays the part of a senior companion in the same field. The means he uses are the mutual exchange of ideas in discussion, advice from his own experience and that of others, and a detailed attention to the individuality and the personal needs of the trainee. He must not force upon the trainee methodically rigid images unsuited to the latter's own personality; that would be to abuse AT for the sake of mastery over another person and would be moving dangerously close to the sphere of shamans and wizards.

Once the training period is over, the AT initiate is ready to practice autogenic training daily on his own, in the privacy of his home or office, alone or with one or more friends.

II

THREE PREREQUISITES

Experiments into the applied physiology of the sympathetic nervous system, of which AT is an example, call for optimal experimental conditions. Choosing a time and place, finding a suitable position, and beginning with a largely conscious, deliberate stage of relaxation are essential requirements. It is also necessary always to end the sessions with the same routine, which should be mastered before beginning the exercises proper.

The time and place for practice

Let me begin by saying that, for group instruction in AT, the room chosen must meet certain conditions. A suitable room for group exercises should be large enough for all the participants to lie outstretched on the floor without getting in each other's way. In many groups the participants sit in armchairs or lie in reclining chairs. Every AT instructor will draw on his own experience and will use what he has found to be most helpful. I myself leave it to each individual in the group whether he prefers to sit or to lie down, if he has already had some AT instruction; but I make a point of having beginners lie down. The reason seems simple to me: a supine person has the least difficulty in relaxing completely.

In individual instruction I proceed as follows: in the first session I give introductory information about AT and then let the trainee demonstrate his usual lying position—the position he finds most conducive to relaxation. Starting from this position, I lead him to a relaxed supine position which he can maintain for a short period, even though he would normally prefer a different position (for example, on his side with arms and legs uncrossed and his back slightly curved—the fetus position). The relaxed supine position has the legs slightly separated, toes falling outwards, elbows flexed with the arms beside the body, and the head, with or without a pillow, centered on the axis of symmetry. This is the position of a person lying relaxed as if ready for sleep. In my experience, almost anyone can do AT for a few minutes in this position. But I do know of a few exceptional cases: some women show a need to let their toes fall inwards rather than outwards; they describe this as taking a strain off the inside of the thighs. In such cases, I fall in with any reasonable wish, provided there is a noticeable improvement in the degree of relaxation they attain. But by far the most common variation is the fetus position described above.

Besides being large enough, the room should be comparatively quiet. Rooms at the back of a building, away from the street, or cellar rooms if available are the most suitable. The room should also be screened from glaring sunlight and have its own indirect lighting. These conditions are not always easy to find in group instruction, but in any case it is essential that there should be no direct disturbance from outside. It has been proved that a loud noise outside on the street is less of a disturbance than the unexpected presence of potential intruders immediately outside the door of the room. It is a good idea for a person practicing at home to put a note on the door and to arrange with the family which room he will be using and thus prevent being disturbed. Then a trainee need only say that he is now going to do his training, or to put a prearranged sign on the door. It is very hard to cope with a really unavoidable disturbance, such as the ringing of the telephone, if the trainee knows that no one except himself is there to answer it. He is advised in the first session calmly to conclude his training session as soon as the telephone begins to ring and then answer it; it should not take longer than three or four rings to get to the phone. He must regard the telephone as an external object rather than internalize it as a device that disturbs him by interrupting his exercises.

Finally, the room itself should not be warmer than is normally found comfortable. Overheated rooms are not suitable for AT. Ill-ventilated, smoky rooms are also unsuitable, as are those that are too cold. In individual sessions of a few minutes' duration, a cool, well-ventilated room can be used, provided the trainee has a light blanket to throw over his feet and legs. His arms should remain outside the blanket.

The question of time has been given a lot of attention in individual as well as in group instruction. There is no general rule for the times for AT, but it is important that each person should establish some sort of routine which he can maintain and which will facilitate regular practice over the weeks and months. Everyone must find a niche in his routine for two brief sessions daily. From the point of view of the psychology of learning, the integration of these practice sessions into one's normal daily routine is of inestimable help to the actual process of learning AT.

For those who work full-time, it is advisable to find a spot in the morning getting-up routine for the first session. In most cases it is a good idea to do this after rising and dressing, using the now-cool bed. However, the training can be done in a different room on a suitable couch or, in fact, on the carpet in any convenient room. It is important that the lower half of the body be covered by a light blanket. A person beginning AT needs the instructor's help in choosing the best time in his morning routine, and a detailed discussion of the trainee's personal habits is essential.

The prescribed second daily session, which both the beginner and the advanced trainee should make every effort to observe, should be a time in late afternoon or early evening which fits easily into the rhythm of his working day. Here one must take into account when the trainee leaves work and how much time, including the time for the evening meal, he has at his disposal between leaving work and the beginning of his evening leisure time. It is best to fit the AT session into this period, though one must remember that a session should not be scheduled for the period of extreme fatigue immediately after reaching home. I would recommend in most cases that the person rest for ten minutes first, then do something reasonably distracting like opening the mail or reading the papers or a magazine. Then, he should go to his usual place for his exercises and have his session before supper. If trainees complain that they are very hungry when they get home, obviously this must be taken into consideration, but a snack is quite enough to alleviate the hunger feeling. It is not advisable to have one's session when one is feeling full—a full stomach has no room for AT. Similarly, a session while very hungry or thirsty is not to be recommended.

Once established, these practice times must not be seen as rigid necessities. The trainee must realize that the observance of set times is a great help, but it can be an even greater help not to insist on one's routine but to be able to adapt to one's surroundings. This can be the case if the person is traveling or is visiting where he can vary his routine and adapt it to the circumstances he finds.

For particular professional groups, the time factor must be treated quite differently. For example, a housewife will find it more convenient not to include her AT session in the early morning routine, which is always a bit of a rush, but to wait until the family has left the house, when she can enjoy a longer training session completely undisturbed. The same may be true with the afternoon or early evening session: it can be most conveniently fitted in before husband and children arrive home, while the woman still has the time to herself.

Other times present themselves in the case of persons with an irregular daily or weekly schedule. General rules are hard to formulate here. The guiding principle common to all of them should be to make a virtue of necessity, i.e., to turn the accidental and irregular features into an essential characteristic of the training. To take an example: a traveling salesman who covers several hundred miles a day in his car and spends every night in a different place, in different hotels, could most suitably devise his own opportunities before his morning departure and after reaching the evening destination, arranging himself for a training session with the help of a blanket which travels with him, and lying on the carpet in any room. First he will arrange the room suitably, shutting windows against noise, turning down the lights, and ensuring that no one will come in. When he has done this he can use the same routine for his sessions every day quite independently of the varying rooms, and thus train just as regularly and successfully as a person in his own home. The precondition is the establishing of a voluntary attitude characterized by pleasurable feelings. And here indeed is the point at which one can tell whether a person regards AT as a burden that has been put upon him or is freely taking advantage of a possibility that is open to him.

Still on the subject of time, there is one thing that should be said about sessions in unfavorable circumstances, in the presence or proximity of third parties. I can refer only briefly to this problem here, because sessions carried out under extremely adverse conditions presuppose complete mastery of the technique in a sitting position. I am thinking here of those who cannot choose the times for their sessions and, in their professional lives, must take advantage of every opportunity to make time for a session. The classical example for such difficult circumstances is the executive, tired from conferences, or the wage-earning worker bound to strictly observed working hours. Here I advise trainees to make a habit of an additional or replacement session, to retreat for a "quickie"; this is possible for all people under all circumstances: in the bathroom. A visit to the toilet is accepted by everyone, and anyone can count on a secure three to five minutes without being disturbed. With mastery of the training in a sitting position—and the lid of the closed toilet makes an eminently suitable seat—he can carry out his training without fear of interruption. People whose lives are hectic, their working days filled with incidental occurrences, can in this way make time for frequent regeneration of energy through AT.

One final word on the question of time and place: everyone should learn, at the beginning of a course, to approach the instructor with details of his own experiences and observations in such matters as soon as the problems arise, or when difficulties that have been ignored threaten to gain the upper hand. In no case should anyone try to struggle on in the face of present difficulties or obstacles. AT does not succeed through this kind of conscious desire or by battling against the odds.

The best position for training

The best position for training is the one that best suits the individual. It is helpful for the instruction and learning of AT that most people are able to lie in a relaxed position with legs outstretched and slightly parted, the feet falling loosely outwards, arms flexed beside the body, and a pillow under the head. A few do feel extremely uncomfortable in this position, and it would be misguided to force them to adopt it. Some people prefer a different position, such as the fetus position; one can learn AT equally well in that position. A patient and tolerant understanding in the case of such individual wishes relieves the learner of much difficulty and effort. Whether the trainee sits or lies is, from the point of view of the teacher, quite immaterial to the actual acquisition of the method. The trainee might find his first attempts in AT succeed more readily if he is able to take up a comfortable position without difficulty. The majority of people have no difficulty in familiarizing themselves with their first training experiences lying flat on their backs.

In both individual and group sessions, I regularly proceed by asking the person or persons to demonstrate how they themselves lie most comfortably. I then lead them to a questioning self-criticism, correcting uncomfortable positions which I bring to their attention by suggesting they experiment with other positions. It will not do, for example, to try to correct a favorite arm position by direct instruction, not to say admonishment, especially if the position looks as if it had been prompted by self-consciousness or embarrassment.

In response to this first invitation, many people lie on their backs with their arms folded under their heads. This position should not, however, be criticized, as most people will then defend it as being extremely comfortable. It is preferable to ask them to experiment, just for the fun of it, and try to find other positions that are just as comfortable. Almost automatically they discover that to have the arms at their sides, slightly flexed, is much more relaxing. And now the first explanation can be offered. The instructor shows that by raising the arms above the head and folding them behind the head, the shoulders are drawn up, the upper chest is constricted, and respiration becomes more difficult.

It is equally simple to convince beginners that folding the hands across the chest is by no means a relaxing position. But in this case too it is not advisable to try to change the position by criticizing it and rejecting it; a sympathetic invitation to try another position is more successful. A person can accept an explanation as helpful only after he has discovered for himself that having his arms loosely at his sides provides a feeling of well-being across the whole of the chest because he can now breathe more freely. Everyone simply has to admit, after such an experiment, that to have the hands folded on the chest, with a tendency to drag toward the elbows on either side, means that there is a weight pressing on the rib cage. The result is that the hands themselves must be tense in order to maintain the position. The hands and forearms, through their weight on the rib cage, are an obstacle to relaxed breathing and exert an uncomfortable pressure in the region of the heart. The beginner must experience this for himself.

Once the right position has been found, it is a simple matter to interest the new trainee in the fact that he has discovered this position only after overcoming certain inner resistances. It is helpful here to begin at the head. He is asked to maintain his position but to let his head roll gently from side to side like a ball and to observe the state of his neck muscles. Many tensions become noticeable. Some of them can penetrate to awareness before the start of AT proper, and these can and should be allayed by conscious relaxation techniques.

Next come the shoulders, which as a rule are drawn up without the person being aware of it. In order to draw his attention to this, I ask him to draw up his shoulders still further; I suggest that he try to draw them all the way up to his ears (which of course is impossible). Once he has reached a taut position with his arms stiff and his shoulders drawn up as far as possible, I instruct him to let them down quickly, to let them drop to his feet. The result is surprising. He reaches a more relaxed position than he had at the beginning of the exercise, and he experiences the relaxation he would not have been aware of without this invoking of the extremes.

In the same way, the beginner is asked to become aware of his arms, the contact of his back with the floor, his hips; to gyrate his pelvis to find out whether or not it is at right angles to the horizontal axis of his body. When he has this awareness of his arms and trunk, he is asked to visualize his legs as hanging loosely from the pelvis and, like an athlete, to loosen them up further by shaking them a little, and then to lie still.

These preliminary exercises at the beginning of AT enable the trainee to learn to draw on aids that, of themselves, do not belong to AT. The gymnastic loosening-up which everyone is familiar with, either from athletics, dance, or exercise classes, should be regarded as a preliminary aid to accessibility and should be presented with the aim of creating the necessary preconditions for AT.

At this point, the actual training can begin. But before learning the method of achieving the trancelike state, the trainee must be taught how to "return" from the trance safely.

The perfect return

The term *"zurücknahme"*—"return," "resumption," or "withdrawal"—is of Schultz's own coinage. It denotes the deliberate, self-directed termination of the AT session by the trainee, and is of particular importance even to the beginner, because one cannot tell from his appearance to what extent he has already intuitively reached, even in his first days of practicing, a very deep experience of relaxation from which he must, like the more experienced, find his way back to a normal "ready-for-action" state of muscle tone and nervous system. And he does this with the aid of a special technique. "Return" means a return to the normal ready availability of all one's limbs. It is very important if one is to avoid having one's actions or more complicated muscular movements impeded by some residual uncertainty or weakness.

Goethe's *Sorcerer's Apprentice* teaches us that a technique, once learned, must be countered by another equally effective technique if things are to return to normal—though of course in the case of AT we are not dealing with magic, even if it does bring about remarkable changes.

The return is described in Schultz's teaching pamphlet as follows:

> The return should always be carried out in the following way:
> 1. the arm is stretched and flexed a couple of times, energetically, with a sort of military jerk;
> 2. a deep breath is taken and then exhaled;
> 3. the eyes are opened.
>
> Or in the form of a formula:
> 1. Arms firm
> 2. Deep breath
> 3. Eyes open

Experience has shown that these return formulae lead many people to perform a very strenuous, even violent gymnastic exercise, which cannot really be advisable. Anyone who has watched people perform their return with violent jerks and tremendous muscular effort, stretching their arms and legs, breathing strenuously, and tearing themselves with a mighty jump out of a state of complete limpness and relaxation must fear the worst. One other modification, the so-called Bavarian return, which involved a pleasurable stretching like that of a person who, after a deep sleep, is having trouble finding his way back to reality, does not pay due heed to the physiological demands which the return must satisfy. However, I will not pass judgment, as I have seen such trainees reach very good results with their training. On the other hand, I see no reason why I should teach such modifications of what are really simple instructions.

The form I recommend for the return is based on the fact that the totally relaxed, limp neuro-muscular apparatus should, with a little help, revert pleasantly refreshed to its original state, and the trainee should feel calm and full of inner strength. To achieve this, it is necessary, as with the entry into the AT state, that the hands and arms—as parts of the body with the preferential function as the representatives of the ego in the cerebrum—should take the lead. In detail it is as follows:

While still completely relaxed and supine, the trainee closes both hands to form fists without any discernible further muscular activity; he clenches them so tightly that an observer or this instructor can tell, by the whiteness of the knuckles, that the fist is clenched as tightly as possible. These clenched fists, which usually lie nails down, knuckles up, beside the body, are then rotated outwards from an overhand to an underhand position. Keeping them parallel, the trainee then draws his forearms slowly and forcefully upwards, becoming pleasantly aware of the flexing of his biceps. When he has drawn his forearms up completely in this pleasurably energetic way, he rotates his fists again so that they now face outwards, thumbs in. He then stretches both arms slowly and forcefully. The result of this is that the chest expands involuntarily. Once the arms have reached their original position at the side of the body, he automatically feels a need to exhale forcefully and with pleasurable relief. He should then relax the tension in both arms, preferably while still exhaling. If he finds it necessary, he may then do pedaling exercises with both legs. Finally, he opens both eyes and then, in a leisurely manner, he sits up and remains for a few moments in a sitting position.

The whole procedure falls into three operations:

First, the body regains control of the voluntary musculature, as exemplified by the arms, which demonstrate the recovery of our command of all the voluntary musculature.

Second, in consciously regaining the vigorous use of both arms, the trainee becomes aware in a very elementary way of his return to a strong, healthy state of being no longer tensed up or harassed. The regenerative effect of AT is evident in this attainment of a conscious feeling of strength.

The circulation is now switched over to a state of activity. Hence, thirdly, the unhurried trainee sits up and remains briefly in a sitting position before standing up.

The upshot of all this, even for the inexperienced, is the realization that lavish movements and violent jumping up cannot provide the qualitatively beautiful experience of taking control of oneself, nor can they lead to the well-regulated circulation (adaptation effect) that is desired. A return involv-

ing a sensible expenditure of strength over a small distance,
under the constant control of one's own awareness of the
growing strength in one's fists, forearms (in the rotating of
the fists), and upper arms brings a new bodily awareness
which, through the contrast with the bodily awareness of
complete relaxation in AT, offers a real step forward as far as
elementary self-awareness is concerned.

Every trainee should ask his instructor, who has mastered
and is teaching this technique, to demonstrate it in detail.

III

THE COMPLETE BASIC TRAINING

The so-called basic stage of AT is the original, the "real" AT. The name basic stage was coined only after J. H. Schultz had developed what is called the advanced stage, which will be discussed in a later chapter. I have already, in other publications, taken exception to the rather unfortunate distinction between the basic and the advanced stages, since this must provoke value judgments which are quite out of place in any consideration of these two complementary methods. The basic stage of AT is a complete and independently practicable method. Whether, why, and under what circumstances a trainee should augment it with the advanced stage is a completely different matter.

In the course of the presentation of the so-called basic stage that follows, let us not then lose sight of the fact that this method is complete in itself and forms a unit, even though for practical purposes, individual parts of it must be discussed separately and independently. The individual parts of the basic stage are usually called "standard exercises."

Schultz preferred to call them *"Einstellungen"*—"orientations"—and I too prefer this word.

Setting the mood for peace

Structurally AT starts with a concrete goal. The suggestive
power of this goal cannot be overestimated and furthermore
can be considered objectively in any evaluation of the method
itself. The trainee is invited to assume the position he finds
most comfortable, sitting or lying down, and to check his relaxation with a few quasi-gymnastic trial exercises. He is
then instructed to concentrate on the thought "I am at
peace."

This is where the first problems arise for many beginners,
problems which I think are unnecessary and easily avoidable.
Proper presentation and a helpful introduction should ensure
that those who are very ambitious and achievement-orientated
do not see this instruction as an imperative which calls for an
immediate increase of effort. The mood formula "I am at
peace," also referred to as the peace formula, is nothing
more than an invitation to surrender oneself unreservedly to
this thought. Anyone who is used to letting his thoughts run
as his fancy leads them, or to turning his imagination to a
freely chosen object or topic, will find here simply a new
content for his imagination. Those, however, who suffer
from an inability to concentrate must of course expect to have
their usual difficulty here. To this extent, the beginning of
AT plunges in at the core of the difficulty of concentrating
on a chosen theme at any given time; hence the eminently suitable description of AT as "concentrative relaxation."

Beginning AT should not cause the trainee to struggle against himself. Unfortunately this does happen in the case of unsatisfactory instruction in AT, and it often presents an insuperable difficulty when people try to learn the method without a teacher.

The peace formula is a motto for the whole undertaking. It makes good sense to put the goal at the beginning, usually in connection with the possibilities which can be derived from the content of the goal. The motionless supine or sitting person can have no more appropriate thought than that his cerebral activity is relaxed as well and that his concentration is, for the moment, focused on nothing further than this state of peace. Admittedly this procedure harbors a paradox which cannot be overlooked by anyone who has seriously and successfully tried to master AT. And the resolution of this paradox is the immediate goal of the first two weeks of training.

If the beginner concerns himself, during his twice-daily short sessions, with the fact that he is outwardly relaxed and inwardly at peace, this limited goal enables him to place himself at a distance from all mundane matters and to gain a certain intimacy with himself. To experience the fact that a peaceful posture results in a state of peace is the "homework" for the first week or two. During the first instruction session, the length of which depends on the circumstances and the particular needs of the trainee, one can talk about practical matters such as the three prerequisites of Chapter II. At the second session, the experiences of the trainee can be discussed. With that starting point, the instructor can broaden and deepen what he has to say, and can give the trainee the helpful confirmation that his first independent experiences constitute a good beginning.

I cannot say too often that the communication of the for-

mula ''I am at peace'' is not a command and not an attempt
at deception. The peace formula does not preclude the fact
that the beginner may well feel anything but peaceful. Everyone at some time or other has his mood disturbed by external
or internal unrest. The success of the whole endeavor does
not suffer because of this. But it would be greatly to the detriment of AT if the trainee, either at the beginning or later,
were to get bogged down over the frustrating experience that
peace is never, in actual fact, as beautiful as he can imagine
it. The goal still remains the same. His actual concrete experiences are not going to be measured against some absolute
norm of peace, but are to be focused anew each time on the
same constant goal. When the beginner is dismissed after the
first session with these instructions and with recommendations for his own practice sessions at home, he is like
someone who is learning to swim. The first thing demanded
of him is that he entrust himself to the water, which up to
now has not carried him. The swimmer must first learn that
the body does float; the trainee must experience that peace
does come if peace has been outwardly established and inwardly conjured up.

Keeping notes on one's own first attempts as requested by
the instructor is very important and can subsequently be very
fruitful. The introduction to the peace formula is closely
linked with a reassuring and explicitly encouraging promise
that concentrating on ''I am at peace'' will set up a resonance
within the trainee; he does indeed let it happen, and then
writes down what he has experienced. All my case material
from the past fifteen years bears witness to regularly occur-
ring peace experiences, of varying intensity and number, as

recorded in the notes of the first weeks. There are of course also reports that peace was not to be found. The risk of concentrating on peace even when disturbance or distracting thoughts force themselves upon you is unavoidable. But these risks are also responsible for the first successes, which are to be valued the more highly because they arise from the trainee's experience of himself.

It is necessary to mention one particular disturbance that may occur at the beginning—not an actual physical disturbance, but thoughts of various kinds, banal or irrelevant ideas. To try to steel oneself against these and banish them by an exercise of will power would contradict the whole intention of AT. These unbidden, irrelevant thoughts need not be fought, merely calmly put aside—or even better, saved up for later. A helpful formula here is the friendly attitude "fine, but not now, later; it's AT now." The trainee can then repeat the peace formula mentally and attempt to resume his practice. He soon finds that irritating and distracting thoughts stop of their own accord, and soon cease to occur.

To make the self-experience of AT more vivid to the reader, I present below, and where relevant at the end of subsequent sections, a sampling of notes which some of my pupils have taken on their first AT experiences with the various standard formulae.

"I am at peace"

"Feeling that I am on the surface of a great depth. When I breathe out, often the twitching returns, or the beginning of it. Sometimes a sinking out of the darkness. Feeling of weightlessness, with the sensation of a gentle, uncontrollable turning which disappears as soon as I focus my thoughts on it.''

"First my body relaxed, then an inner distance to myself, tingling. Surroundings are far away. No sense of time. Joyful mood.''

"I am aware of my borders. There is a pulsation in my extremities; I know where I stop.''

"Head still heavy, eyelids pulsating. Suddenly I had the feeling I was lying in a hammock swinging back and forth. Had to laugh, told myself I could laugh later, did the exercise again, and a third time. After about five minutes I had to laugh again and returned.''

"In front of my eyes and nose, deep down, a feeling of heaviness which at the word 'completely' [1] led to a sensation of expansion from narrowness to wideness.'' [This trainee drew in his notes a wave with the words "I" and "completely" on the crests and "am" and "relaxed" in the troughs.]

"It took quite a while before I felt really relaxed. At first, for some time, a funny trembling between my closed eyes and my forehead, about the middle. Then I had a feeling in the fingers of my right hand that reminded me at first of heaviness and was then as if the fingers no longer belonged to me. As soon as I noticed it, the feeling vanished but then it came back in waves about three times more. Once I felt the same thing in my left hand, but not so strongly. My legs seemed to twitch a few times at first and then they just lay there as if they weren't a part of me. My breath became quiet and regular. However, it did bother me that I had to swallow twice in the first third of the session. Toward the end, my right eye opened three times without my wanting it to.''

---

1. The German peace formula is *"Ich bin ganz ruhig,"* "I am completely relaxed"; "I am at peace" is the English version used here.

"My hands ended up like under a veil. Arms and hands seemed to be far away, for some moments as if they were asleep."

"Relaxation of the tongue muscles. Body heavy. Pleasant feeling of relaxation."

The working arm

The first two of the six standard exercises or orientations of AT are concerned with the realization of physical experiences in the periphery, particularly the arms and legs. Heaviness and warmth are experienced in the limbs, but at the beginning are not felt in all the limbs simultaneously, although this is the goal of these particular exercises. For reasons deriving from the psychology of learning and from the neurophysiological structure of the human body, work on the experience of heaviness and warmth begins with the hand and arm which the trainee normally uses: right-handed persons practice with the right hand, and left-handed persons with the left.

There are very good reasons for this. The human hand and arm are particularly well-developed organs and they are correspondingly well represented as to size and structural detail in the cerebral cortex. Man, unlike the other higher mammals, has special large cortical areas both for motor activities and for sensory experience. Man has a large motor and sensory-speech center, and a similarly large center, in another part of the cortex, for his working arm. AT is based on an anatomical-physiological phenomenon which Schultz called "the generalization of the experience of heaviness and warmth": when alterations in muscle tone (heaviness) and vascular tone (warmth) are registered in the particularly large area of the cerebral cortex that corresponds to the trainee's preferred arm, the effects automatically spread to neighboring regions of the cortex.

The practice of AT takes advantage of these simple facts. The trainee practices heaviness and warmth in the right (or left) hand and arm. He then waits for the generalization effect. There are preferred pathways along one side of the body, and other forms of extension which tend rather to a symmetrical effect in the other side of the body.

These basic facts of anatomy and physiology decree that heaviness and warmth must be practiced strictly with the dominant arm. The trainee should wait until generalization occurs—and no one can predict whether he is going to generalize along one side or symmetrically.

In group work, the facts about generalization can be mentioned and explained as far as necessary, preparing the group members to discover their *own* generalization effect. One method which must be condemned as showing a disregard for this simple matter of nerve structure is that of having trainees practice right and left arm and leg successively. This kind of training is really a step backwards into a heterosuggestive quartering of the trainee and thus robs AT of one of its own best possibilities. Once the trainee has had his own first experiences of heaviness and warmth it should be his own personal further experience that the generalization springs from within himself, autonomically; through it, he should come to a deeper awareness of himself.

Not surprisingly, a method such as AT must reckon with the possibility that in response to the formula ''right arm heavy,'' a trainee will occasionally experience heaviness in the left arm, or even in both legs. It is one of the great advantages of AT that such an occurrence, if spontaneously communicated, can be taken up and integrated into the course. This example—heaviness in the left arm in response to a formula for the right—can sometimes reveal an unsuspected left-handedness. It is then advisable to change the formula and to allow the trainee to give all his exercises a left-hand orientation. As for the example of heaviness in both legs as the first spontaneous reaction to the formula "right arm heavy," there are many possible causes for this, but we can leave them undiscussed for the moment. The instructor should assure the trainee in question that his response is not wrong by any means; on the contrary, it is very good indeed and that he should continue to practice with the formula as originally given in the expectation that heaviness will manifest itself throughout his body, including his right arm. Such premature generalizations or jumping to other parts of the body are entirely harmless as long as the instructor is able to deal with the understandable anxiety and bewilderment of the trainee. In all cases, however, the exercises should begin on that side of the body where the dominant arm is.

As you can see by studying the following notes, often the feeling of heaviness does not come right away, but after a short delay. Note words such as "sinking," "leaden," and "lying firmly on the floor" to describe the eventual feeling of heaviness in the dominant arm.

"Right arm very heavy"

"Experienced heaviness in right arm but had hoped for a more distinct sensation. Afterwards very relaxed. AT only partially successful with the experience of heaviness but very helpful in relaxing after an exhausting conference.''

''After the preliminaries, heaviness came at once and grew stronger during the session and was the strongest sensation so far. It spread to the rest of the body, particularly in the right arm a strong impression that the arm was lying firmly on the floor.''

''A lasting sensation of sinking, leaden arm. Gradual relaxation of the shoulder muscles, waves of the warmth in the arm, heaviness in the right arm.''

''I was reflecting on whether I had any response. In the middle of this exercise I came back into my mind— and suddenly I felt for the first time a positive heaviness and relaxation in my legs which up to now I had only ever had in the arms. So I stopped the session there, feeling very satisfied.''

''Experience of heaviness particularly strong in the right leg. Then a disintegration of the heaviness from the fingertips up to the shoulder. Heaviness in the right leg comes automatically and a stronger feeling of warmth in the right side of the body.''

''Arms heavy—again the feeling that I am submerging under some sort of covering.''

''Heaviness at intervals in the right arm, and then calves and left arm heavy.''

''Reached relaxation quickly and without interruption. I am not really clearly conscious of the right arm as heavy. What is stronger is the feeling of contrast with my left arm, which is lighter and 'higher.' ''

''The inner quieting down of my body comes on faster now. After a few exercises, my right arm felt heavy. Right arm and hand seem to be longer and thicker. This feeling extends to the right side of my chest. The whole of the upper half of my body on that

side seems malformed. The whole body, especially arms
and legs, is heavier. Now the whole exercise seems to
do me good. Afterwards my whole body is quieter and
more relaxed.''

"Found peace quickly. My arms felt very heavy.
Imagined I was Götz von Berlichingen—not just with an
iron hand but with an arm that was pressing right
through the couch.''

Discovering heaviness and warmth

With a good initial experience of peace as a foundation, the
experience of heaviness is normally localized in the right
forearm, confirming the formula quoted above, "right arm
very heavy.'' This centering of the experience of heaviness
in the right forearm is in keeping with our anatomical-
physiological makeup, which we can refer to in understanding how this subjective experience of heaviness in the
body or limbs comes about. Even when relaxed, each limb,
and the trunk to an even greater degree, still maintains
enough muscular tension to hold the position the body had
taken up. Under the influence of progressive relaxation in the
trance state of AT, when the muscle tone is decreased still
further and causes a loosening of the joints, the receptive
centers of the sensory organs register a state of yielding,
sinking, or lying more heavily on the respective surface.
Translated into terms of naïve experience, this results in a
sensation of heaviness.

Thus the experience of heaviness is "real.'' When a person is relaxed, this relaxation does not necessarily penetrate
the consciousness. Only through the inward repetition of the
formula and through the AT process as a whole and the

trance state it induces can the relaxation be made available to
consciousness. The heaviness conjured up before the mind's
eye is already present, but it is only now actually *experienced*
as heaviness. This is why I use the expression "the discovery
of heaviness." Popular notions of relaxation exercises in general and of AT in particular suffer from the misconception
that an experience such as heaviness is one which the subject
is talked into or which he talks himself into. This notion is
partly to blame for the failure of many techniques and is an
obstacle to success with AT.

Heaviness can, as I have said, first manifest itself in other
parts of the body; it is not tied to the invoked right (or left)
forearm. Normally one would assume that heaviness would
first become apparent in that part of the body which offers the
best conditions. In some cases this will have the effect that a
part of the body which is already greatly relaxed—affected
by the autogenic trance—will be the first to signal heaviness
and will thus seem to be an island of heaviness within the
body.

From time to time, trainees report sensations of heaviness
which later turn out to have been quite different feelings. For
instance it is not a sensation of heaviness if the position of
the head is registered as being uncomfortable. True, the head
is heavy and it presses against whatever it is lying on; but the
trainee is not supposed to become aware of his head as
heavy. What he does feel, in such cases, is local pressure on
the skin at the back of the head. Such perceptions which lead
to mistaken impressions can easily be removed by cushioning
and raising the head a bit with a pillow. There is a similar
difference between a true sensation of heaviness and reports

of legs "heavy as lead" at the beginning of AT. I know from experience that such early reports usually indicate poor circulation, sluggish veins, or other purely physiological troubles with the legs. Heaviness is essentially a pleasant feeling related to remarks about similarly pleasurable feelings of tiredness.

Ever since the early days of AT, trainees have been offered helpful hints to improve their results with this formula. These are not really necessary, but they can have a supportive function for some trainees. Here, however, we must distinguish between aids of a visual nature with a strongly heterosuggestive character which force upon the trainee an image that he himself might never have come up with, and aids which can be easily assimilated into his own ideational and experiential world.

Two examples will serve to explain what I mean. Images of an arm heavy as lead or of an arm in a plaster cast seem to me unsuitable. The use of inorganic, body-alien imagery makes it more difficult to come to an experience of oneself. If a trainee, however, hits upon such an image spontaneously, one can consider letting him use it if it obviously improves the result. The image of an arm carrying a heavy basket could, for example, be helpful in discovering a feeling of heaviness. But on the whole this image is not to be recommended, as there are many people who have no first-hand experience of carrying burdens with their arms bent.

These examples show the need for much intuition by the instructor and for an intuitive response from the trainee if AT is to be really productive. The imaginary aids to the realization of heaviness sometimes arise, much to the surprise of the instructor, from completely different spheres. I would like here to mention, as an example, a painter and decorator who took up AT because he stuttered, and who was able to over-come this handicap completely through being able to free himself from the overpoweringly strict influences of his childhood and youth. It was a striking feature of this case that the patient's results with the warmth formula improved greatly with the unbidden image of an invisible hand in a railway carriage that switched the heater from cold to hot. This patient had obviously been able to transfer the effect of powerful and invisible authority figures to a positive experi-ence of beneficial warmth. This strikes me as being a remark-able instance of sublimation through inversion.

And thus we have come to speak of warmth and must, right at the beginning, concern ourselves with one fundamen-tal difference between this and the heaviness formula. Heavi-ness is, in essence, quantifiable and could be increased up to a theoretical maximum degree. Warmth is different. An un-hindered increase of warmth leads physically to something which is no longer felt subjectively as warm but as hot. And here it becomes a question of quality rather than quantity. Warmth as a sensation is beneficial; it is sought, it revives, it protects. Heat is avoided; it is felt as unpleasant and it is dan-gerous to life. The same is true of its physical opposite. Cold is dangerous, life-destroying, and unpleasant, in contrast with coolness, which refreshes, enlivens, and has pleasant emo-tional connotations.

This must be seen as a basis for the experience of warmth. A second precondition is inferred from its more subtle mani-festation. Heaviness was exemplified in the whole arm because the three joints—the shoulder, the elbow and the wrist—provide through their varying angles a sensation of heaviness by means of the specific sensory awareness of depth. We were thus quite justified in using the whole arm to gain access to heaviness, which then later spread to the rest of the body. But warmth is of a more subtle sensory quality. It must be focused on a smaller area. In addition, in everyday experience the arm is normally covered by a sleeve while the hand is vulnerable to the temperature contrasts of the air for much longer periods. A third factor is that the warmth sensors are much closer together in the hand than in the upper part of the arm, to say nothing of the rest of the body. Taken all together, we can see why it is sensible to begin the practice of the warmth formula with "right (left) *hand* warm."

It should once again be noted that the unquantifiability of warmth, which is associated with comfort only within narrow limits, forbid the inclusion of the word "very." Schultz drew attention to the delicate interplay of vascular regulation from the very beginning and always warned against overdoing the introduction to the experience of warmth. This further supports the reduction of the formula to three words.

The discovery of warmth in the right hand is often accompanied by other physical sensations and by the occurrence of certain spatial experiences. The warm hand is felt to be enlarged or swollen. Not infrequently the experience of warmth is preceded by concomitant secondary experiences; from these, we can see that the experience of warmth is not imaginary but the very real effect of greatly improved blood circulation in that part of the body. Seen in this way the sensations of tickling, prickling, pins and needles in the fingertips, and a swelling of the hand are not surprising. The experience of warmth in the hand is a subjective awareness of better circulation, and this is the goal of our efforts at this stage of AT. Better peripheral circulation and an increase in warmth induce a feeling of comfort and at the same time actually improve one's physical state.

With warmth too, as with heaviness, it often happens that it is not the limb mentioned in the formula but some quite different part of the body that first signals success in the exercise. And what we said about a discussion between the trainee and the instructor concerning heaviness is equally valid here. Once warmth has been discovered and can be found regularly after one or two weeks of regular practice, heaviness and warmth can, in the course of a normal session, be practiced with an eye to a complete generalization of both. But the experienced instructor does not insist on this inflexible scheme. He takes up suggestions from the trainee with regard to other physical sensations which I will discuss systematically in the next section. I myself have had great success with the principle that the organism and the personality of the trainee must be taken seriously as a guide to the course of the training. If individual variations in practicing do not actually contradict the fundamentals of AT theory, I give them preference over any rigid plan of instruction.

Warmth often manifests itself in parts of the body where it does not arouse pleasurable sensations. This is regularly true of warmth in the upper part of the neck and the face. A beginner must be helped here, so he will be able to cope with an uncomfortable surge of warmth to his neck and face. One step is always correct here: to break off the session as soon as unpleasant responses are registered and to try again later. Among the unpleasant and unexpected reactions to the first attempts with the warmth formula are contrast experiences: instead of the hand or hands feeling warm, as intended, the feet may feel cool or even cold, frequently colder than before and sometimes as cold as they were before the start of the session. Many people suffer from cold feet, sometimes from cold hands as well. And it is obvious that AT, which can be so beneficial in precisely these areas, must not be allowed to fail because of this difficulty. As long as the distracting contrast experiences occur before successful generalization, there is a well-tried, flexible routine that can be used to anticipate spontaneous generalization by means of a strictly focused orientation to various parts of the body successively. Only in this one case and at this point at the beginning of the course do I depart from my principle of waiting for spontaneous generalization. Without deliberately introducing practice on all four extremities one after the other, which I criticized above, I do permit a careful practicing on hand and feet alternately, but stress that the dominant hand must be focused on with preference and should, if possible, always be the location of the first warmth experience.

Aids to discovering warmth are perhaps even more popular than those for heaviness. Various authors mention again and again the helpful effect of a warm bath for the hand or arm before beginning a session. And we have the anecdote of how Schultz used to introduce a cat which sat on the forearm of the trainee and, purring loudly, transmitted its warmth to the arm. I have never used such props myself, but sometimes I find it helps to mention casually that the trainee should imagine he is lying out of doors in such a way that the sun is shining on the limb in question, the right hand. To improve results as a whole and to prevent an unnecessary further cooling out, I insist that the trainee cover his feet and legs up to his waist with a light blanket. Those who begin a session with cold feet should in any case remove their shoes and tuck a blanket around their feet so that the improved circulation that results from this cozy wrapping with no constricting footwear can warm them up.

Although heaviness and warmth are presented in this order, it often happens with the heaviness formula that an experience of warmth is registered first and that the heaviness does not manifest itself until later. This is of no importance to the success of the course as a whole. Anxious trainees who fear they have done something wrong can be reassured by being told they have not.

Finally, one most effective aid must be mentioned which is closely connected with the physiological basis explained above. If the warmth formula proves difficult, the formula can be extended to read "right hand *pleasantly* warm." One further modification of the formula may in rare cases be necessary when, on the formula "right hand warm" there is a massive, oppressive, or unpleasant warmth response, or even surges of warmth. In such cases we can either retain Schultz's method of repeating this formula three times only, or we can choose to phrase it as "right hand *slightly* warm." Later the formula can be reduced to its original form, or it can remain as it is for this particular trainee *only,* and become his standard formula for all his training.

The following are samples from my students' notes on this exercise.

"Right hand warm"

"Almost immediately a general relaxation and then feelings of heaviness and warmth in my left arm and leg. Left hand warm. Tickling and twitching. The latter in right and left arms. No sensation of warmth but an indeterminate awareness of temperature, like when you touch a very cold piece of metal and cannot tell whether it is cold or hot. Slight tingling in the skin and hand."

"Realized what it means to let go. Together with heaviness my inner relaxation increased. Hand warm fairly quickly and with it heaviness seemed to be flowing in waves through the arm and hand."

"The feeling of warmth in the skin in the exercise 'right hand very warm' remains even in a cold room."

"The formula 'right hand warm' brought about a strong, pulsating feeling of pressure in gigantic hands. For the first time had the feeling that I was experiencing something very beautiful. 'Right hand warm' caused an intensive but still pleasant feeling of pressure, especially in the fingers, but without their size increasing—as if they were about to burst."

"With the warmth formula first a feeling (especially in the hand) that everything is expanding and getting wider. My arm feels stronger. The feeling of heaviness increases, but not really warmth. After further practice even stronger effects, particularly in both forearms and calves."

"Warmth in both hands perceptible very soon, spreading only slowly to other parts of the body. Only weakly in the legs, but instead a peculiar feeling in the thighs and arms."

"I don't really feel that my hands are warm, but I am aware that that they are. My own formula: 'right hand nice and warm.' "

"Feeling of warmth in the right hand, the rest of the

body heavy. Simultaneously with the warmth in the hand I can feel the blood pounding in my fingers.''

"Very relaxed, strong feeling of heaviness and a perceptible feeling of warmth.''

"Warmth and heaviness in the whole body, somewhat dry mouth, tummy rumbling.''

Generalization

The generalization of the experiences of heaviness and warmth that were first attempted with the dominant arm is the goal of the first third of AT and is the foundation for a superior sort of total generalization known as the organismic shift. Every well-devised course of instruction should be geared to this goal. Now we can regard these manifestations of heaviness and warmth as a whole and once again stress the more important instructional aids.

With the experience of heaviness, there occurs a partial generalization effect with the establishing of symmetrical heaviness in the arms and legs. But this by itself is not the generalization that we are aiming for. The trunk as a whole, and most perceptibly the back and the lumbar region, must participate in the generalization. This must always remain the individual experience of the trainee and it cannot be systematically advanced by any further formula. I have learned from experience that there is no point in introducing special aids for the back at this early stage of AT. According to the standard method of J. H. Schultz, no formulae are intended here. The back, the lumbar region, the chest, and the pelvic region participate in the generalization by themselves. The responses of the trainee follow shortly and usually sound like this: ''I feel broad and heavy . . . weighing on the bed, sofa, floor, etc. . . . My body is sinking further and further into the mattress . . . as if I were being pressed into the sofa.''

Sensitive guidance in AT by a responsible instructor forbids anticipating this total experience heterosuggestively. The reason for this, as I see it, is that with any given trainee such a massive, obtrusive interpretation of the state he is supposed to be in could very easily be introduced at an inappropriate time, or too early, so that he is overwhelmed by it and might even feel that he is being pressed down from above. This could hardly occur without causing anxiety. In the usual course of AT sessions, one always reaches these or similar experiences of the self and, if the trainee has discovered them for himself, they will be characterized by a feeling of happiness and palpable success. Heaviness, when generalized, intensifies the experience of peace, and peacefulness in turn influences the experience of heaviness. Thus the first major unity of physical well-being is attained.

Sometimes, instead of feeling heavy, there is an inversion at the beginning: the trainee feels that he is floating, raised up from the mattress and incredibly light and unburdened. Should this be the case, the trainee should be told that he has not done anything wrong, nor has anything gone wrong. The sensation of being raised up or of being euphorically light is only verbally a contrast to heaviness. As far as muscular relaxation and the lessening of muscle tone are concerned, as is obviously the case here, the trainee has achieved complete success; it is just that the translation of this into subjective experience has somehow produced a contrasting image. This must not be allowed to confuse the trainee. It is important to realize that the signals for total relaxation of the muscles and joints can sometimes be those of pleasant floating sensations.

Asymmetrical responses at the generalization stage are always of short duration and do not impede the further course of the training. If such experiences crop up in notes or are reported during a session, the instructor should explore with that individual why one portion of the body is preferentially experienced as heavy. A clarification of this question can sometimes bring into consciousness interesting details from the experiential world of the trainee. Heaviness, and occasionally lightness instead of it, do not, in my experience, remain long as alternatives. Every trainee quite quickly finds his own stable and easily reached total experience of heaviness.

The generalization of warmth can only be sensitively observed and improved by supportive explanations by the instructor. But when both hands and, from the hands upwards, the arms up to the shoulders and finally the whole upper part of the body are felt to be warm whereas the legs and especially the feet remain cool or cold, specific aids are called for.

J. H. Schultz told his pupils to help such persons to "send the warmth down into their feet." The individual instructor must turn this recommendation into a practicable aid. It seems necessary here to avoid the most obvious formula "both feet warm," and instead to proceed as follows: the trainee continues to use the formula "right hand warm" and waits for the generalization in the upper half of his body. He then repeats "right hand warm," tries to imagine warmth as such, and directs his gaze toward his feet without altering his position. Without changing the standard formula, the feet are thus included as part of the body. Looking toward one's own feet integrates them better into the general awareness of one's body and thus draws them into the experience of warmth. If a satisfactory warming of the feet is still not achieved, I usually just go on with the course because, when dealing with the body formula, "solar plexus glowing warm," there is a further opportunity for the extension of the warmth experience. Using the solar-plexus formula together with the idea of feet, into which warmth is visualized as flowing from the pelvic area along the thighs and calves, the effect of warmth in the feet never remains absent for long.

Warmth is the subjective experience of improved circulation. So it follows that with the help of a successful standard exercise for the circulation, the warming of the periphery should improve. In stubborn cases we have one further possibility besides the standard formulae, which in my opinion should be used only when all the aids I have mentioned up to now and the combinations of various formulae within the first phase have still not led to the desired result.

Even at the beginning of a course of training, an undesirable spreading of warmth to the neck and head sometimes occurs. At the stage of the warmth and heaviness formulae, the only really effective means of combatting this is a prompt return. It follows from the structure of AT that a reliable shielding of the neck and head area is possible only after the sixth standard formula has been learned. This sixth formula, coolness of the forehead, also effectively encourages a better warming up of the feet because, with the polarization of the awareness of temperature in the contrast between the cool forehead and the warm feet, a further experiential effect takes place. But I will return to this question in greater detail when I come to the section on the cool forehead.

Peace, heaviness, and warmth—the latter reliably and speedily generalized—are the core of AT. Many trainees find in these fundamental exercises sufficient help for their symptoms, their particular difficulties, or their general tenseness. A training that unites the periphery and the trunk in equilibrium and awareness of temperature with a generalized deep experience of peace can be effectively used in treating certain disorders of the sympathetic nervous system. I think it a very good arrangement for this immediate goal to be proposed for general courses and for the sessions to be arranged so that the trainees direct their efforts toward it and attain it. A further course can be added at any time and AT completed once such an effective, if limited, grounding has been achieved.

The inner rhythms of life

The formulae that now follow in the basic training, those for circulation and respiration, are quite different from the fundamental training in peace, heaviness, and warmth which we have been discussing; they bring the trainee into a new relationship with himself. But before I discuss these two formulae in detail, there are a few questions common to both which should be raised.

A well-structured preliminary training which can call at will upon a feeling of peace and a generalized awareness of warmth and heaviness serves as the basis for observing one's pulse and breathing, which lead to experiencing the rhythmical processes within the body. The inward-focusing person, relating only to himself in undisturbed peacefulness, warmth, and heaviness, manages as if automatically to hearken inwardly and to become aware of his own vital rhythms. The normal process of AT provides an array of evidence that the trainee, even before he is acquainted with the following formulae, has already had sporadic or even regular sensations of his pulse and is aware of his breathing as peaceful. The early occurrence of the experience of pulse and breath is a good measure of the depth and quality of the training up to this point.

Everyone knows from his own experience that, given peace and quiet, he can hear a watch ticking and other even less obtrusive sounds (which had previously been drowned out). It is not really any different with the awareness of one's own pulse and breath rhythms in the state of relaxation that exists after the progress from peace through heaviness to warmth. Both these formulae concerned with the body's vital rhythms intensify the experience of peace. The breath experience leads, during exhalation, to an intensification of heaviness. The awareness of one's pulse in the periphery, particularly in the fingers and toes, improves the degree of warmth in that moment when the pulsation becomes noticeable.

Pulse and the experience of circulation

Schultz expresses the third formula as "pulse calm and strong." Even in later editions of his book there is an illustration of a trainee with his right hand laid over his heart so as to feel his heartbeat. After many discussions of this means of reaching an experience of one's heartbeat, and as a result of my own experience with patients, I have arrived at the modification that one should not become aware of the heart in isolation. My practice is to explain to my trainees the connection between heart, arteries, capillaries, and veins and to define the pulse as a heartbeat which is propagated into the most extreme periphery. After such instruction I leave it to the trainees to find their own experience of their circulation. It is completely up to them in which part of the body an individual is to have his own experience of the pulse.

The equal value of all pulse experiences must, of course, be assumed. And we must realize that the heartbeat or pulse is different in different individuals and that it is always felt in that place which is particularly disposed to it. For instance, nervous patients may report that a heartbeat which at first was strong and forceful calms down in the course of a session. Others report a pulse experience in the large arteries near the surface, for example in the neck, temple, elbow, or knee. Still others notice their pulse first as a fine pulsation in their fingertips. Not a few report that they feel a sort of beating in their body, which is quickly explained as the pulsation of the aorta, the main artery.

No matter where the pulse manifests itself, it should be registered according to the formula as calm, at the very most as strong. It is never permissible to include an indication in the formula with regard to the frequency of the heartbeat. This is important for many people because, although a rapid pulse is an expression of their hypersensitivity and nervousness, they can find it upsetting and take it to be a serious symptom of illness. Naturally a doctor could convince a sensible person that the pulse is determined by a complex inner regulatory system and is always adjusted to guarantee an adequate supply of blood to every part of the body, including the internal organs. In AT the trainee should learn by direct experience, not by direct instruction, what is healthy, harmonious, and thus "good." Through incorrect instruction or a sloppy learning of AT, it sometimes happens that the word "slow" creeps into the formula. A directive for a slow pulse contradicts the structure and the goal of the method.

A suggested deceleration of the pulse can, in certain circumstances, endanger one's life and must never be attempted! The heart is a self-regulating organ which adjusts its volume per minute and its pace according to the impulses it receives from a complicated system of signals concerning the amounts and proportions of oxygen and carbon dioxide in the bloodstream. A double safety mechanism and regulatory system ensures this autonomic heart action and it must not be interfered with.

If an AT trainee in a state of generalized heaviness and warmth still has no sensation of his pulse, this third formula is a suggestive aid to discovering his pulse experience. The goal of the organismic shift and the deep relaxation in AT does not presuppose any other qualities for the pulse experience than harmonious peace and a regular heartbeat. This crucially important section in the discussion of AT perhaps makes it clear that the responsible teaching and therapeutic use of AT should be in the hands of an experienced doctor.

I believe the practice of the cardiac-circulatory experience in this basic stage proceeds best using whatever spontaneous suggestions the trainee made during his experiences of heaviness and warmth, or when he first registered a pulsation or, specifically, a heartbeat resonating against the front wall of the chest. From this point on, one can practice with the intention of becoming aware of one's pulse in other parts of the body. This is a seeking of the pulse without any particular intention. If the experience of warmth has been unsatisfactory or sometimes seems to weaken and ebb, the pulse experience, once learned, can be directed to the hands and fingers or feet. This leads automatically to an improvement of the warmth experience through the improved circulation.

The conscientious taking of notes on one's own experiences offers better possibilities for making the very real effect on the regulation of the body convincingly clear. Simply through the weight of the arm itself, the hand laid on the heart can, in many cases, cause feelings of pressure and even anxiety. I have been convinced by my own trainees that the autonomous experience of the heart beating regularly or of the pulse in various parts of the body gives a powerful insight into the regulability of the autonomic functions of the body.

The standard formula, "pulse (heartbeat) calm and strong," can in some cases be varied. Some trainees report that they experience their pulse or heartbeat as uncomfortably strong and are thus distracted from the rest of the AT experience. Such an exaggerated concentration on the circulation, possibly coupled with feelings of anxiety or vague restlessness, must of course be counteracted. Usually dropping the word "strong" from the formula is enough and, for a further intensification of the experience of peace and a totally effective manifestation of harmony, using the word "regular" instead. Roughly speaking, people with poor circulation, dizzy spells, and a tendency to low blood pressure can use the standard formula as it is. But more active types, people with high blood pressure, and people who tense up easily should use the modified formula with the word "regular."

Here are some examples of trainees' notes on pulse.

"Pulse calm and strong"

"Heaviness and warmth both achieved promptly. Perhaps I don't notice the onset of the feeling of heaviness very well because it is there from the very beginning. I can always feel the width of my back and the relaxed resting of my body on the bed. Pulse has the best onset: at once and throughout the body."

"Toward the end of the session I can feel a clear hammering in my fingers. Although peace and heaviness come quickly I still feel very light. Again at the end, a brief hammering in my head, especially at the temples. The hammering in the fingers seems to be stronger. Now that I have changed the order of the exercises, putting breath earlier, I am more aware of my heartbeat. Right over to the right side of my chest. Now I feel the heartbeat more clearly in my head and my hands too. This and the previous exercise seem very similar to me. My body becomes more tranquil in this exercise. I feel particularly relaxed and light, so that the heaviness that came at the beginning of the session is hardly perceptible any more."

" 'Heart and pulse calm and strong' makes me feel as if I were sitting up to my neck in a tub of comfortably warm water and it was making me feel good."

"Heaviness and warmth quickly, then pulse in the belly."

"Heaviness and warmth promptly. Pulse first in the fingertips, then around the feet and ankles. Later in the temples and finally around the stomach."

"A calming beating of the heart."

"A strong pulsation; I can feel my skin from within. Later pulsation at the back of the neck."

"Pulsebeat in my right hand, a slight feeling of pressure from the couch against my arm."

"Heaviness and warmth good. Blood beating in hands and feet. Heartbeat clearly discernible."

"Pulse calm and easily noticeable in fingertips, right wrist, and also in the throat and the back of the head."

"What is really noticeable is the calming down of my heartbeat from the beginning to the end of the exercise."

Breath—not a breathing exercise

This fourth standard exercise or orientation is a special case. Whereas the previously attained experiences of heaviness, warmth, and pulsation are without any real rivals, the AT trainee, in learning the breath experience, is often confronted by obstacles that must first be cleared out of the way. There are so many different kinds of breathing exercises that one cannot keep track of them all. The value or lack of value of each method can be decided only in individual cases. The AT trainee must accept unconditionally from the very beginning that the formula "breath peaceful and regular" is not a breathing exercise and must refrain from trying to influence his breathing deliberately, or he will prevent his own access to the experience of breath. This breath experience occurs spontaneously in AT at the very latest when the relaxed, supine trainee, in a state of generalized heaviness and warmth and in possession of the experience of his pulse, repeats to himself the formula "breath peaceful and regular."

This may sound facile to the skeptic. The simple explanation is that the trainee, through his state of inward absorption and relaxation, has in the course of his bodily experiences begun to breathe peacefully and regularly long since, but without becoming aware of it. In AT, one's breathing becomes *consciously* peaceful and regular only when one turns one's awareness to it and permits this self-experience of breath. Through the first weeks and months this self-awareness is intensified by means of the autosuggestive qualities of the breath formula. And with days and weeks of breath experiences behind him, the experienced trainee can recall his breath.

Nothing occurs when practicing the breath formula that has not occurred in the case of the previous formulae: the trainee's relaxed, inward-oriented attention finds his breath, which reveals itself to be as the formula had stated. Should he at that time be insufficiently relaxed, the suggestive power of the formula will enable him to relax. After a period of discovering this awareness of self which intensifies his relaxation through the breath formula, he is able to find access to this extremely beneficial experience regularly and without difficulty.

J. H. Schultz has characterized the state of the trainee who has found the experience of breath in the now-famous complementary or substitute formula, "it breathes me." This statement is more a kind of confirmatory, concluding definition. Dilettantes both with and without instructors have been forced to realize how misguided it is to take this formula and make it the goal of their efforts. "It breathes me" cannot be used as the suggestive formula necessary at the beginning of the breath experience since, compared to the standard formula "breath calm and regular," it is nonvisual. Those who have not yet discovered their calm and regular breath cannot summon it with the formula "it breathes me." For the inexperienced the "it" is conceptually and contextually too vague. Experienced trainees can use the "it" formula if they like, in place of the standard formula. Very experienced trainees who are far advanced in AT do not need rigid formulae at all, but rather accompany their training sessions, which begin and end almost autonomously, with brief cues: peace, heaviness, warmth, pulse, breath. For finally, the experienced trainee proceeds with his training intuitively, without conscious thought and, as a result of his having mastered the process in a strictly schematic way at the beginning, he finds all the experiences automatically in the sequence that bears the stamp of his own identity.

Only at first, then, does one need to reckon with any difficulties, particularly if the trainee has had disturbing previous experiences with other breathing exercises which attempted to regulate his natural breathing either through his own will power or in response to another.

In AT the breath is not influenced. Its harmonious rise and fall, physiologically the result of its even regulation by the respiratory center of the cerebral cortex and controlled in detail by the chemoreceptors at the fork of carotid arteries, is merely experienced in the state of relaxation that has by then been achieved. In the course of training, breathing that is possibly not yet quite regular can become more so with the help of the autosuggestive formula "breath calm and regular" and then be subjectively experienced as such. It is precisely this transition from the less peaceful to the completely peaceful, regular breathing which often provides the trainee with an illuminating experience of entering the AT state, intensifying the relaxation throughout his body.

It is the task of the instructor to help remove difficulties wherever they occur and indirectly to offer help to those who need it. If a trainee has not been able to reach a contemplative, direct experience of his respiration, it is better to guide him toward other related and harmonious concepts than to keep him concentrating on his breath, where his voluntary efforts are causing a blockage. Although in general I do not use many directly visual aids, I would recommend to a beginner struggling with difficulties that, while constantly repeating to himself the standard breath formula, he should imagine treetops swaying gently in the breeze, or try to recollect pleasant hours spent lying in the bottom of a boat and rocking gently with it, feeling the light swell of the waves and hearing the regular sound of the waves lapping against the shore.

Attentive trainees who keep careful notes and wish to intensify their training have repeatedly confronted me with a question which I would like to discuss in the context of this section.

Anyone who remains in the breath experience with perceptible feelings of comfort observes after a while that his breath has become slower, and that the inhalations have become shallower. Then suddenly there is a great need to draw a deep breath. Those who have mastered AT give in to this inner urge only to notice a great deepening of the experience of heaviness and then they immediately fall back into their previous breath rhythm, which continues to bear them along. More timid souls suspect an irregularity and want to know the cause.

Peaceful and regular respiration is the result of a long period of breathing at approximately the same tempo. The respiratory center maintains this rhythm until the chemoreceptors signal a deficiency or oversaturation of oxygen in the blood. A reduction in oxygen and an increase in carbon dioxide cause, so to speak, a correcting of the respiratory clock. After this correction, which is subjectively felt as a need to take a deep breath—which includes both a vigorous inspiration and a relaxed, pleasurably passive expiration—the breathing rhythm continues with the same regularity as before. The notes illustrate this point more accurately than further description could do.

"Breath calm and regular"

"Good relaxation, much warmth, and regular deep breathing."

"Movement of diaphragm very clear, noticeable belly breathing, and with it increased feeling of warmth in the legs."

"Did the session very peacefully. Very relaxing even after the negotiations. The association that my head is rising a bit on the word 'breath' and sinking back on 'calm' is very helpful."

"Immediately calm breath, swelling of the calves, a bit of pressure in my head, but then relaxed again and a feeling of warmth throughout my body."

"Breathing in intervals, like those with the formula 'right hand very heavy.' I fall into this rhythm automatically."

"With the breath orientation I often feel an intensification of the other orientations."

"Stayed a long time on breath. I have the impression that my observation won't interfere with the sessions any more."

"On breathing out, a feeling that air was streaming into my abdomen."

The "mini-training"

Since the AT trainee does not have a couch or carpet at his disposal everywhere and at all times, I would like to mention a few of the possibilities of AT which are not connected with the supine position.

AT is sometimes taught in a sitting position. Those who practice lying down should also familiarize themselves with AT in a sitting position and sometimes use it. I have left these questions of method and technique until now because a trainee who has mastered the first four orientations, assuming he has learned them lying down, can learn the new positions more quickly. He will, however, also notice that training while seated (or standing, in some situations) is not just a variation or a second-best, but can greatly extend his training and the use he makes of it.

Sitting

There are two sitting positions which must be distinguished: leaning back in an easy chair with a high back and a headrest, and sitting upright on a stool or straight chair. AT can be done in either position.

Granddad's wing chair. Today there are high-backed chairs to suit every taste. Our fathers enjoyed the comfort of a well-upholstered chair with a high back and winged headrest for their midday nap or for the peaceful days of their retirement. This apotheosis of Spartan comfort still survives in trains where, against the monotonous sound of the wheels, one can practice AT extremely well. What a boon for weary commuters!

Any chair, provided it is not too soft and not too long in the seat in relation to one's thighs, can serve the purpose: AT in a sitting position needs a comfortable seat with firm springs—one should not sink into it—arms that do not wobble, and a backrest. Backless seats, if they are otherwise suitable, can simply be placed against the wall. Cushions for head, neck, arms, and back can be added at will. It is obvious that AT in an easy chair is not so very different from AT on a couch. The body is bent at an angle of roughly ninety degrees to the thighs, the lower legs bent downwards at approximately the same angle. Supporting the legs with a leg-rest usually makes no great difference, but in some cases it can vary the position considerably.

In his transition from practicing AT only when supine to occasionally practicing in a chair, the trainee will notice a fairly clear shift in the tenor of his experience. He can make great use of this through his notes and through talking with his instructor and his fellow trainees. Among the most common changes reported to me are those concerned primarily with the experience of heaviness. The arms are now noticeably hanging from the shoulder joints and the underarms resting heavily on the armrests. The heaviness of the legs can benefit from this new position too. In the experience of warmth it is now often easier to channel a disturbing flow of warmth away from the face. The experience of heaviness in the trunk does not change so much quantitatively as qualitatively, which is easily understandable.

Intensification through alternation. According to the basic physiological law by which sensory images are most clear when they are either beginning or ending and less discernible in a state of constant stimulus, a systematic and deliberate change in the position used for practice can bring about a marked intensification of the subjective experiences and ultimately of the objective results—not just in the initial phases but for the whole course of training.

The cabby's slump. Most people are familiar—mainly from illustrations—with the dozing cabby. This exactly describes the position for AT on a seat without a backrest. Unfortunately, not all who try AT in this position are successful. "The dozing cabby" should convey a relaxed position which older people know well from the days of horse-drawn vehicles and hansom cabs. The cabby, waiting for a customer, sits slumped forward, sleeping or dozing on his box, which of course has neither a backrest nor adequate armrests. J. H. Schultz recognized in this unsupported sitting position the spontaneous regulation of equilibrium—possible even on a moving vehicle—in a state of dozing absent-mindedness, light sleep or even intoxication, of a person whose external stimuli were negligible and monotonous. Schultz made use of this observation for the technique of AT.

Passive equilibrium on a stool. No one today is able to learn the AT sitting position simply from being told he should sit like a cabby, because this has become meaningless today. For this reason I prefer not to use this description in teaching. I would rather help my trainees to become aware of the gradations in their search for equilibrium on a suitable stool. This is why I do not introduce this position until the fourth orientation at the earliest, so the trainee need not have his first experience of heaviness under adverse conditions (compared with the optimal supine position). His own experience of heaviness in his arms, once mastered lying down, is then integrated into the practice session while sitting.

A well-balanced sitting is something people must see demonstrated. The essential thing is that the center of gravity of the whole body is located in the pelvic region. This cannot be achieved by merely bending the upper body forward and passively resting the arms on the thighs; this leads only to further constricting the body.

One particular opportunity of practicing AT in the "cabby slump" is available to everyone—on the toilet. Many years ago Schultz recommended an undisturbed session in the bathroom to all those who find no other opportunity in the course of their working day. Since then I have advised all trainees who need a short break at school, office, or factory to carry out a short session on the toilet.

Standing

An abbreviated training with selective relaxation of the neck and shoulders region goes back to Schultz too. For this it is necessary to stand with the legs slightly apart with the shoulders brushing the wall behind you. The eyes should be shut only if the trainee is absolutely free from vertigo. The arms hang relaxed at the sides. The formula is: "I am at peace—breath calm and regular." The exercise in standing, which should only be done for brief periods, is very useful in any case of tiresome waiting. I myself do it when I have a short break, as tension almost always first makes itself felt in the shoulder region. But it is also pleasant to be able to recall one's accustomed training session by means of this partial experience in the middle of the working day.

Swimming

One other brief training is particularly enjoyable: the swimmer floating on his back in the water, preferably the warm water of a heated pool, anchors himself with his toes to the rung of the ladder or the side of the pool and holds himself steady with minimal movements of his hands, like a fish standing against the current. The experiences of heaviness and breath combine very well with each other here. When he exhales, the swimmer sinks slightly deeper in the water; when he inhales he rises again—the breath rhythm can be concretely experienced in the rising and falling. In the section on the breath I mentioned the bobbing boat as an aid to regular breathing. The experience of warmth is sometimes universalized for the first time in this water exercise, where the head, being out of water, remains unaffected by the generalization. I know of no experience of the pulse in this rather playful AT variation; probably the breath rhythm is so dominant that the other biological rhythms are obscured in comparison.

The "mini-training" is obviously a matter for unusual situations and is of course of interest mainly to those who have already reached the fourth orientation. It can be seen as a kind of reward for persistence and achievement of AT in the supine position.

The abdomen

In the passive concentration of AT, the abdomen and its organs play an important role in the harmonization of the physiological system. The abdomen is focused on as a part of the body and, through AT, takes its place in the scheme of one's somatic awareness and becomes experienced pleasurably, whereas in daily life we tend to ignore it unless it draws our attention to itself through pain or discomfort.

What is the abdomen? Anatomically speaking, the abdomen is the largest of the three body cavities—the others being the cavities of the skull and the chest—and has a few particular features which are of importance for the further course of AT.

In contrast to the other body cavities, the abdomen is only partially surrounded by bone (ribs, pelvis, vertebrae).

The diaphragm and the floor of the pelvis as its upper and lower muscular limits contain respectively its entrance and exit.

The front wall of the abdomen is made up of connected muscles; their participation in the external act of respiration affects the internal organs; like a sort of press apparatus it effects the voiding of body wastes and the expulsion of the baby at the moment of birth.

There are many organs within the abdomen which are regulated as a whole through their regional autonomic centers from a sort of central signal box: this is called the solar plexus. AT for the human being as a totality demands the inclusion of the abdomen in the training. The abdomen in all its complexity of morphological and functional detail becomes the focus of a dynamic experience of warmth in AT by means of an orientation to the solar plexus.

"Solar plexus warm." It is not difficult to manage this formula successfully, but it does demand more insight into the physical construction of the organism than was necessary in the case of the mastering of warmth and heaviness in the limbs.

First of all, the trainee must have some idea of just where

his solar plexus is. But since people other than doctors and nurses have learned AT including the solar plexus formula, it obviously does not require any detailed knowledge of anatomy to be able to focus on the correct part of the body when practicing the formula. General aids to orientation (". . . two fingers above the navel, behind the stomach . . .") have proved less useful than a simple directive to the trainee to find the center of his body, the solar plexus, which, though not outwardly marked, can be experienced from within.

Those who want to know in more detail can turn to an anatomical atlas. There they will find that the solar plexus, together with a network of other plexuses, lies in front of or beside the aorta and thus in front of the projecting upper lumbar vertebra—all in all, an impressive complex of nerves and ganglia. The solar plexus is visible only after most of the intestines have been removed. The transfer of this visual impression into the self-awareness in a state of progressive training can cause some difficulties. Sometimes the trainee gets the depth wrong and focuses too far back, or he underestimates the distance and gets stuck in an attempt to realize an experience of warmth directly beneath the belly wall. The correct focus is achieved without conscious thought, from within, "there where my middle is, deep within me—solar plexus warm."

The formula. Anatomy and physiology teach us that the solar plexus governs the activity of all of the abdominal organs directly or indirectly. It was, then, a simple and inspired deduction that led J. H. Schultz to revitalize the abdomen through the solar plexus by directing warmth to it. Subjective warmth is, objectively, an improved flow of blood: this is the converse of our experience with peripheral warmth in the limbs.

The formula "solar plexus warm" evokes more than just one response from the organism. A subjective, very pleasant feeling of warmth in the middle of one's body is the direct response. This can but need not occur. Indirect responses in great number frequently occur before the feeling of warmth. They arise through the successful innervation of the organs through the solar plexus. The abdominal organs respond in their own way, thus announcing their very existence for the first time. Hitherto unrecognized pain, spasms, sluggishness, constipation, and unhealthy bloatedness can come to consciousness for the trainee. In the process of relaxation one becomes aware of existing tensions.

The formula "solar plexus warm" expresses with the utmost succinctness everything that can be experientially achieved with regard to the harmonious dynamics of the abdomen. As a result of the organismic shift, there is probably a noticeable intensification of intestinal activity, tangibly and audibly, for the trainee as well as for the others present: tummy-rumbling and gut-gurgling unmistakably confirm that the plexus formula has "taken."

Next in line are involuntary, imperative responses to the invocation of the solar plexus, such as the need to empty the bladder or move the bowels. Occasionally, a sexual arousal is reported, often culminating in orgasm and involuntary ejaculation for men.

A confident, prompt and, in serious cases, patiently persevering session with the plexus formula helps intestinal colic, gall bladder colic, and ailments of the urinary tract. A mastery of AT, focused on the solar plexus, is beneficial in childbirth. Women who have learned AT have shorter labor than others.

The abdomen as an enclosed space. The abdomen as space comes to consciousness through its borders, which in the main are voluntary muscles, and thus the rediscovered vitality of this part of the body finds its expression in the flexibility of its walls. Next to the experienced mobility of the diaphragm, the awareness of the pelvic floor is most important. For women, this brings deeply personal experiences of the body in connection with menstruation, pregnancy, and childbirth. Men should focus their awareness on the exit from the pelvic cavity. Both men and women need a firm center for the awareness of their bodies.

Whether one has a lean belly or the ample curves of a rounded tummy, from the point of view of the solar plexus, the belly walls are not rigid and are capable of being felt from the inside, especially when a peristalsis—a wave of contractions—flows along these walls.

Only an intensified familiarity with the plexus formula can bring about an experience of the inner physical structure of the body as a cavity with depths and borders. Together with the experience of breath, the body experience of the abdomen provides an inner knowledge of the diaphragm, extending to the barely definable feeling that one is present in one's own body. In contrast to our knowledge that man breathes through mouth, nose, and windpipe, we are filled with an apparently paradoxical awareness of "exhaling into the belly cavity."

Here is our confrontation with the limits of the explainable and the approach to the irrational nature of the ultimate inner experiences man has of himself—in a state of autohypnosis. It remains—and perhaps always should—indescribable with words.

"Solar plexus glowing warm"

"Everything there. Warmth from the middle of the body outwards and back again. Like a great bowl."

"Solar plexus: slight growling in my stomach, a feeling as if my belly were collapsed like a deflated balloon."

"At first, pressure on my stomach again, then my hands turned into paws and combine with the belly to form a great unit. This reminds me of pictures by Botero."

"With the plexus formula my belly grew very lively. Surface sensations on the belly, not reported in detail." [When questioned: a clear apprehension of the contact of the skin of the belly with the clothing.]

"At the plexus formula a surprising but very pleasant tickling in the thighs. Warmth flowing to the feet and back. Head slightly perceptible. Afterwards easy and relaxed. Legs loosened and circulation in the legs good."

"Pulse concentrated on the stomach area. I can feel the pulse going deeper and deeper, oddly enough like a chemical reaction with gas bubbles rising slowly to the surface. For a short while I felt as if there were two broad bands around the kidneys, but I can't describe the feeling. They run like parabolas, rising toward the shoulders, and stop before they reach the spine. Deep relaxation."

"At 'plexus glowing warm' I can feel warmth behind the wall of the stomach; it seems to be good for the digestion. Rumbling in my stomach."

"Feeling as if the belly wall were being tickled on the inside. A variety of experiences within the belly: a veritable concert: Good session."

"Feel a pleasant warmth in the belly and in the thighs. Stomach growling."

The head

The sixth formula completes the basic stage. From this point on, the trainee is here seen as a whole in a state of autosuggestive trance. Without the plexus formula and without the "cool forehead" formula, AT would still be a useful relaxation exercise centered on the arms and legs, accentuated in the pulse rhythm, and lulled in the breath rhythm, but it would be a limited experience. The added dimensions of the final two orientations complete the experience.

Cerebral activity for AT, the effectivity of reason and will power, began at the beginning of the training with the peace formula. The trainee gained access to AT; by temporarily blocking out his intellectual processes and learning to concentrate on circumscribed parts of his limbs, he secured a reduction of muscle tone and general vascular relaxation through the generalization effect. This generalization extends to the torso. The experiences of the vital rhythms of pulse and breath focus the self-awareness; they open the way to the abdomen where the pulse felt in the abdomen and the participation in one's breathing allow the trainee to find the center of his vitality.

AT must not remain mindless, but the rational mind, the reflective brain, continues to remain uninvolved. A head that does not think but is aware of itself as present can be drawn into the deeper relaxation. And this is effected by the formula "forehead pleasantly cool." Schultz spoke of a "cool, de-concentrated head" and gave his students and patients this image to visualize: lofty subtropical snowy peaks, like Kilimanjaro or Fujiyama, enthroned above lush warm regions of rich vegetation.

Cool, not cold. In all the warnings against exaggerated or wrong use of particular formulae which Schultz repeated with unflagging patience, he was most concerned about the proper intention and achievement of the cool forehead. Cold imagined on the forehead can have very unpleasant consequences for the trainee. My experiences with trainees and patients who use this formula carelessly or irresponsibly confirms in every case the importance of thorough instruction. The forehead, as the representative part of the head, and at the same time as the ideal practice ground for a subtle vascular exercise, can and should be imagined as only cool. Headaches, even migraine in predisposed persons, are often the result of improper experiments.

Sunshine and shade. As a support in cases of difficulty with warmth in the hands I have always recommended to trainees to imagine their relaxed hands as being in the sunshine. When trainees going over their notes tell me that in the case of "forehead cool" they had no response, I make a similar suggestion. I confront the trainee, who is fully conscious during the conversation, with the image of himself, in summer at noon, walking southward with the sun in his face until he notices that the other side of the road is shady. He crosses the street and, stepping into the shade, experiences that which is intended by the formula. This transition from warm to cool is elementary, and close to his own experience. At this level of existential experience the head becomes a passive, receptive part of the body. The head does not think; the forehead feels.

> *"Kopf kühl, Füsse warm*
> *macht den besten Doktor arm."*
> (Cool head, warm feet—
> that makes the best doctor poor)

As soon as the cool forehead has been achieved, it can be used to improve the warmth in the feet. When all six orientations have been mastered, they can be practiced in pairs, by turns, for mutual intensification. In this use of contrasts and in the establishing of polarities, the trainee brings about that ideal of healthy well-being which the German proverb so aptly expresses.

Following are some trainees' reactions.

"Forehead pleasantly cool"

"Forehead felt cool from time to time, but I do not really know whether this was not a draft, although there could not have been any in the room."

"Formula 'forehead pleasantly cool' led to warmth streaming into the feet. After this, a perception of a slight breath of air. By see-sawing between the formulae 'feet warm—forehead pleasantly cool' the warmth was comfortably increased. The reaction comes almost instantaneously with the focusing.''

"Forehead pleasantly cool, feet warm, very relaxed, warmth everywhere.''

"My face shrinks, the ears are drawn down, pressure escapes, my head grows clearer.''

"Forehead cool, a feeling of empty space in my forehead. Feet and hands very warm.''

"With the focusing on 'forehead cool,' the pulse that had previously been beating so clearly in my head disappeared.''

Synthesis of the complete exercise

If the training has been followed successfully, the whole is more than the sum of its parts. By this stage at the latest, the trainee actually experiences what he was told at the beginning—or should have been told. It is not superfluous to tell the trainee forcefully at the outset that none of the individual orientations is learned for its own sake. Quite concretely, this means that none of the organic experience in AT can be, by itself, an adequate goal for the training.

Every orientation should be so thoroughly mastered in the analytic-synthetic learning process that the response comes as soon as it is prompted. The immediate reactivation of each partial exercise by means of a brief recalling of the formula or even the imagining of its content in the programed and subsequently retained order can lead to a falling into trance within seconds. The trainee is now "in training" and appears to an observer to be a person in a state of incomparable, totally convincing peace.

"The participant,'' wrote Schultz in his instruction booklet, "must be able, by means of a brief act of inner concentration, to bring about the specific shift at once, so that the body is experienced as a heavy, warm mass at rest with a regular pulse and smoothly flowing breath, and experienced, one might say, separately from the cool, deconcentrated head." To this should be added that the central experience of the self is physical—that is, that it is centered in the body. The "cool, deconcentrated head" is perhaps no longer the thinking head dominating one's naïve physical experience, but essentially it is still present. Its presence, directly invoked through the mastery of the formula "forehead cool," is experienced through a usually pronounced facial heaviness which subjectively feels like a pleasant tiredness and objectively looks like a totally relaxed, rather expressionless face. The lower jaw drops, thanks to the muscular relaxation which extends to the jaw muscles, and for this reason the mouth is usually slightly open.

"The organismic shift"

This expression, coined by Schultz, indicates that the organism as a whole, in a state of optimal muscular relaxation and peripheral regulation of the body temperature, is functioning as a biological unit in well-balanced harmony and is subjectively experienced as such, as trainees again and again independently confirm. Nearly identical reports from many trainees make it clear what we are dealing with is not private ecstatic experiences but, on the contrary, typically human inner experiences brought into consciousness; these were originally part of the experimental capital of the human race but are too often veiled in the active conscious state. Because these experiences are uncovered and made accessible to immediate experience through AT, we may consider AT as a process of self-discovery, a laying bare, differing in method and goals from psychoanalysis. The "organismic shift" raises AT to the level of therapeutic treatment that provides the ego with an experience of self in its bodily identity.

The following notes are eloquent testimonials to the general feeling of well-being and relaxation achieved at this stage of autogenic training.

"I find the exercises so calming and so beneficial that I would like to stay in this relaxed state for much longer."

"The combination of various exercises was again very helpful. I was amazed that I could take the whole training through in six or seven minutes when I usually need ten to fifteen minutes. And still I had the feeling today that it took particularly long."

"Completely relaxed, I feel well. I haven't known such total relaxation for weeks."

"Heaviness and warmth quickly achieved, later an increase in the sensations until I felt that I was completely relaxed, I was hardly aware of my arms and legs. Even heaviness was not really perceptible as such. And my face was relaxed, and my forehead. Warmth in the solar plexus, tummy rumbling and other events that I cannot interpret medically. Once a mild twinge in the lower abdomen, perhaps the urethra? When I got up after the session, I had a pleasant feeling of harmony and gentleness in my whole body. A feeling of physical identity."

"I've only come to notice through the training how

tired or exhausted I used to be, without even being aware of it.''

"I did my exercises four times, with great success. I felt wonderfully fresh for hours afterwards.''

"After AT, a decrease in tiredness. Afterwards I can concentrate better, I'm calmer. I feel really well, and this feeling lasts for a long time.''

"Very tired before starting the session. During it suddenly I had a strange alteration of all my sensations, accompanied by a slight shudder. Images rose before my eyes without the training being disturbed in the least— and then I knew I was asleep. After a while I decided to wake up, and this didn't affect the training either. Feel unusually refreshed when I finally end the session. This session, by the way, did not take longer than usual.''

The scientific basis. The organismic shift manifests itself in a number of measurable processes, events, and states. The relaxed person is unchanged in his personal identity; he forms a more tightly knit entity. The removal of neurotic traits and the regaining of equilibrium in the automatic nervous system evoke subjective feelings of well-being and health. The trainee experiences in himself a neutralizing of the unnatural and the unhealthy.

The practical synthesis. After the "spelling out" of AT in its standard formulae—heaviness, warmth, pulse, breath, plexus, cool forehead—the trainee, now an adept, "reads" AT in a context. When the trainee has achieved a prompt response to all the formulae, he is easily able, once in the autogenic state, to use the various recalled and accentuated orientations to intensify the training and to prolong it at will.

I teach my trainees to do the exercises up to the autogenic shift as a routine—for example in the mornings, when there is little time available, as part of the routine from getting up to leaving the house. Constant practice is necessary for a permanent mastery of any accomplishment. And only if one keeps in form is AT available at all times to dispel restlessness and for the necessary regenerative pause in the course of the day.

Apart from the daily morning session, to preserve one's virtuosity, there should be a somewhat longer training session in the late afternoon or early evening. Weak points can be worked on, favorite orientations indulged in, and the complete AT further extended. During the relaxation in a full AT session, it is important and helpful to combine various orientations with each other, either for mutual intensification or for an effective contrast. In both cases, the training gains in depth, and the risk of floating off into a doze is diminished.

Intensification through combination: four models. The following possible combinations with intensifying effects are well established. We have already discussed the alternation of heaviness and breath as an intensifier for the experience of heaviness. In exhaling, the letting go of air that is seeking a way out, heaviness increases subjectively and this can lead to a feeling, previously unknown, that one is lying deeply embedded in the couch. An experience of heaviness induced in this way has nothing in common with the feeling that a heavy weight is pressing upon the body. On the contrary, this heaviness has the quality of a soft, unresisting sinking into the depths of one's own weight.

Peripheral warmth and pulse are an ideal combination. The connection between peripheral circulation and the experience of warmth is obvious and lends itself to visual representation. The flow of blood into the fingers and toes implies warmth. The opposite finds its expression in a cramplike effect.

Central warmth, flowing from the solar plexus, and peripheral warmth, together or alternately, intensify the experience of warmth and give a feeling of unassailable security.

The experience of breath and the plexus formula in combination evoke a universal experience of the body which is related to an experience of vast space. The torso as a whole becomes an impressive, vast, integrated entity; arms and legs are sometimes temporarily forgotten—which is of no importance as they can easily be brought back to consciousness. If, during this total torso experience, one thinks about one's back, heaviness and warmth can manifest themselves there. The back, that least sensitive region, a *terra incognita* for many people, is a part of the whole and in a complete training should become accessible.

Biological North-South contrast. Warmth in the feet, together with and alternating with a cool forehead, intensifies both sensations. By this means, a barely perceptible sensation in the forehead can be made stronger and clearer, and at the same time the quality of the flow of the blood to the feet can be improved. How beneficial this polarization is can be further seen in the fact that, in the case of certain diseases, from fever to serious post-operative or post-apoplectic states, an artificial re-creation of this healthy polarization must be carried out by means of hot-water bottles and ice packs.

Foundations to build on. In the organismic shift, the trainee learns how to remain long enough in AT without floating into an indifferently pleasurable state, falling asleep, or being distracted. Those who want to go further in AT and to use the method to suit their own personal needs must keep up their training. Trainees have often said to me that on such and such a day the training session went so well that they felt no desire to stop, "I would have liked to go on indefinitely." All very well; but with a little critical skepticism the trainee must surely say to himself that remaining for long in such a "nirvana" is ultimately unproductive.

Since AT is an allowing rather than a doing, and at the same time a productive experiencing of the self, the autogenic shift as an intermediate goal allows one to integrate the so-called intentional formulae and finally the continuation of the training in the meditative projections of the advanced stage. I shall speak of both in the next two chapters, but first I would like to mention briefly one factor of experience that I myself count as part of the basic stage.

Addendum: the skin—conclusions from an experiment

In the section on the "mini-training," I described a short form of AT floating on one's back in the water. When I do this myself I experience a definite relationship with my skin, that organ of the body which, as the outer wrapping, is present all around me and which, like the abdomen, we tend to ignore under the usual conditions of conscious life.

Victor von Weizsäcker was the first, as far as I know, to realize the expressive value of the popular saying *"ich fühle mich wohl in meiner Haut''* ("I feel good inside my skin") for psychosomatic medicine. In functional relaxation (cf. final chapter), the development of this specific experience of one's skin in the sense of "feeling well in one's skin" plays an important role.

We are becoming seriously aware of the skin as an organ and of the fact that the skin has a psychosomatic language of great variety and expressiveness. The physiological function of the skin all over the body is to be the border between the self and the world with which it comes into direct physical contact. It has, of course, the further functions of guarding against infection, regulation of warmth with the help of the peripheral (capillary) vascular innervation, the secretion of sweat, and the integration of the various sensory functions; but these need not concern us at the moment.

The frontier experience inside/outside in the usual medium, the air, is complicated by the problem of clothing and is hard to induce. In the medium of water, where the naked skin, adjusted to a constant temperature, can provide a continuous sensation of contact with the non-self, I became aware of my skin as my "covering." During training on one's back in the water, the combination of heaviness and regular breathing, simultaneously and alternately, provides a basic experience. The extension of the "mini-training" is a matter of an involuntary, barely definable total sensation that I can only describe as "I feel myself represented in my hide." This is a good feeling; it gives a sense of security and is—though not always—connected with a tendency to orient oneself in space.

However, the transfer of these experiences to training

under more usual conditions, naked in a warm room, was not at first very satisfactory. Only with the introduction of a seventh formula, "exterior warm; my borders quiet," could I achieve a similar sensation.

I have had as yet no opportunity to test this clinically. Candidates for such an experiment would all have to be masters of the basic training and be free of skin disease. Only then could one set about the task of choosing a group suffering from chronic skin allergies, teach them AT up to mastery of the basic training, and then, on this basis, work with the intentionally modified formula "borders quiet, exterior pleasantly cool."

The invocation of coolness in cases of itching areas of skin has been known and used since the days of J. H. Schultz. What is here in question is an additional orientation, worked out according to the symptoms presented, in the manner of the intentional formulae or the organ formulae.

The working out of a general skin experience within the framework of the basic training could be a matter for discussion following the results of these experiments. This is another example of the ways in which AT can be expanded and enhanced according to the additional needs and ideas of trainees and teachers in various circumstances.

IV

FINDING YOUR
OWN FORMULA

Since the complete basic training, *qua* self-hypnosis, brings about a controlled, terminable, unusual (non-normal) psychological state, namely a trance, other factors introduced into this state must be checked for their relevance to the trance.

One extension and enrichment of a correctly conducted course of AT is provided by the intentional formulae. These play the same role in AT as posthypnotic suggestion does in hypnosis.

In both auto- and heterohypnosis, consciously directed instructions are incorporated with the intention that they should become effective when needed after the hypnotic session is over. In a state of diminished consciousness, the psyche is receptive to suggestive instructions. In hypnosis, the hypnotist makes posthypnotic suggestions and, before the session is concluded, he instructs the patient to forget that they have been made to him; but he also manages to suggest that these instructions will automatically be followed at the appropriate time.

The self-hypnosis of AT, if it is to deserve its name, works self-critically in proximity with even minimal heterohypnotic influences. It must not be underestimated that the AT instructor, no matter how carefully he controls his words and actions, or how little he attempts to direct the trainee, is still a source of heterosuggestive impulses. The problem with suggestive additional formulae for "afterwards"—whether for the treatment of everyday symptoms, or for work on the inner personality structure and the behavior patterns of the trainee—lies in keeping the heterosuggestive element to a minimum.

Many tried and tested intentional formulae originated with Schultz. Out of a total of a thousand intentional formulae, Klaus Thomas offers some four hundred taken from notes which, because of their good results, could serve as examples for other trainees. According to Thomas, the formulae should preferably be brief, positive, rhythmical, sloganlike, and possibly rhyming or alliterative. On the question whether the intentional formulae should in all cases be positive, Thomas agrees with Schultz in opposing any totally rigid adherence to this rule and concludes that the formulae should be verbalized positively if at all possible.

Preparation

Many years ago, Schultz told a group of his students the following anecdote, which at the time deeply impressed me. I have had much the same experience with my own students and patients. Schultz was asked, "Now that I've mastered AT, what should I do with it?" His answer was brief and to the point: "What's your problem?"

Those who learn AT without the pressure of troublesome symptoms, and who have been drawn to this well-established method because they hope to be able to achieve self-mastery, are indeed confronted at the end of the basic training course with the question "Now what?"

The general benefit of AT consists in the physical economy of effective organic functioning accompanied by a marked relaxation of previously apparent tensions. This benefit is there for anyone who masters the technique and keeps it up regularly. Even "healthy" people whose physical systems are in equilibrium and whose normal behavior is a model of harmony can improve their imperturbability. Persons who had previously felt the lack of this physical and psychological composure profit even more from being able to rely on their mastery of the basic exercises. Most physical symptoms respond to that particular formula of the basic AT which affects either the organ in question or the unbalanced function. In the combination of all the formulae, harmony is improved even in those areas where symptoms have previously been suppressed or negligible. Psychological composure, which perhaps the trainee himself does not even notice at first, develops gradually in the course of regular training even when no direct attempt has been made to reduce his irritability, restlessness, or excitability via the standard formulae. The organismic shift, by itself, has a stabilizing and harmonizing effect in many areas. And disturbances or insufficiencies that then remain are quite suddenly seen as faults, personal failings which one would like to remove but which one had not really been aware of before. Thus there are many more trainees and patients who do not ask, "What should I use AT for?" After the alleviation of the main symptom, they discover that there is something else: "I didn't realize it before. Can I deal with that through AT as well?"

But who among teachers of AT does not know those rightly dissatisfied trainees who, for all their general success and noticeable improvement in their symptoms, cannot rest until they see them completely disappear? Everyone—the happy masters of AT, the eager discoverer of new areas of application, and the partially satisfied—needs the extension of AT. They can all put the intentional formulae to good use.

Six times Schultz, one time Jones. The preparation of trainees or patients for this new section of their training or therapy begins with a brief but striking piece of instruction. The mastery of the complete basic training must be presented as a foundation which will bring about the autogenic shift in all who are willing to learn it, regardless of their individual goals and symptoms. The learning, or better the practicing, of the six orientations of the basic training are the ABC—the introduction, so to speak. My trainees are now told that the time has come to make AT *their* training by adding to the standard formulae (six times Schultz) their own personal formula. And Mr. Jones now understands that he will go on doing his Schultzes but will round things off with a bit of Jonesing.

The intentional formula is autogenic too. My further instructions are limited to encouraging my trainees, in discussion, to describe their individual needs for extension of the method already mastered. Then together we discuss what is needed, what could be improved, and what, in the context of his whole life, might be approached with an eye to change, regulation, or harmonization. After such considerations the trainee is invited to think it over until next time, to have a look at himself and let something suitable occur to him—preferably with the concentrated brevity of a formula.

Commencement. I prefer trainees to become increasingly independent. Our basic concept, conscientiously maintained, is autohypnosis and not heterohypnosis. For me it would be self-contradictory to present the basic training as "autogenic" and then to issue intentional formulae as undisguised posthypnotic instructions. Thus my trainees learn—with some help, of course—to find their own intentional formulae. At the second meeting of the extending training in intentional formulae, the trainee presents his own ideas, plus a certain amount of his own experience, and we discuss this. As no one has ever yet been praised too much but many have been discouraged, I give him as much confirmation, recognition, and corroboration as I can in the light of the circumstances and my own knowledge of him as an individual. Additional formulae thought up by other trainees—their "Joneses"—are rarely usable without some alteration or other. But these spontaneous formulae often provide the right starting point without which the proper, fitting, final formula for this particular person would have been very difficult to formulate.

Whatever the trainee offers, strange as it may be, it is analyzed for its suitability of both content and form. In this way I avoid deluging trainees with recommendations as to brevity, memorability, positive content, and rhythm suitable to a good formula before their interests and personal commitment have had a chance to express themselves or before they have had a chance to think about themselves. At the same time I have been careful not to offer them, much less force upon them, a formula from my position as a teacher. I doubt it is sensible to categorically offer a formula to a trainee or patient and tell him, "take that one, it fits."

While discussing his suggested formula, we also come to speak casually of the important prerequisites which a "made-to-measure" formula must meet—this is a matter of experience. I normally verbalize our formula—the one we have worked out together—presenting it positively rather than offering it skeptically as a matter for further discussion, and suggest that he now use this formula for as long as it remains satisfactory and is not supplanted by any other better idea that may occur to him. I leave it to him to plane it down and even encourage this: the formula is still on the workbench.

Individual formulae—made to measure

The intentional formula, once it has been articulated and accepted as practicable, should formally correspond to the standard formulae and the introductory peace formula, the brevity and suggestive quality of which should be guidelines for the final wording.

But since the individual formulae should reflect the personal needs of the individuals who play a part in formulating them, the call for brevity and pithiness should be presented only as a recommendation which it would be helpful to observe.

Many intentional formulae prove extremely effective even though they are rather long and sound unimpressive on a first hearing. They reveal the personal commitment of the trainee and mirror his continuing inner dialogue with himself. In them, the dynamic thought processes of the individual are revealed. This is more important and more effective than hammering home a resounding slogan which the person might be subconsciously rejecting. Those formulae likely to be acceptable keep to the formal criteria described by Schultz and Thomas and at the same time zero in on the problems of the individual trainee; thus they keep the training dynamic. I remember one example from my days as a pupil of Schultz's which demonstrates this ideal combination.

When Schultz was asked by a very talkative lady, who habitually contradicted everyone, how she should now use AT, she replied to his counter-question "What's bothering you?" that she felt isolated and avoided by people. After a brief period of thought about the cause of this isolation, Schultz gave her the formula, "I hear myself." This can hardly be matched for brevity and memorability. It confronts the person constantly with herself and articulates her own self-criticism. A woman, accustomed to talking, remembers in trance "I hear . . ."; programed as it were for extrovert behavior, talking to others, she simultaneously remembers, in a state receptive to suggestive instructions, the corrective reflexive attitude: ". . . myself."

Off the peg. The first intentional formula is intended to deal with an obvious disorder, a distressing problem in one's relationship to oneself or a conflict rooted in either one's circumstances or interpersonal relationships. Together with the instructor, the trainee works out a suitable formula and works with it. This can go on for weeks successfully and then one day the trainee realizes that, with the help of this formula, he has made recognizable progress.

Depending on the degree to which the trainee has integrated his intentional formula into his regular training sessions, an inner distance is achieved from whatever caused the trouble. Objectively the trouble itself can still persist; but the individual's attitude to it has changed. To give a specific instance for clarity's sake, a stutterer may not have completely overcome his difficulty in articulating words clearly and may not be able to command his flow of speech, but the patient's apperception has changed through the use of such a formula as "breath carries the words." As an integral part of the regular training sessions, a way of speaking has developed which is no longer subject to the constant stress of worried self-control and the concomitant self-imposed "will power," but which is, rather, "discovered" with an increasingly frequent experience of success. The stutterer gains a store of experience which registers in the memory as "it's working—it's all right." However, at this point, an uncritical euphoria threatens to undo the success should all-too-human illusion lead the subject, unawares, to persuade himself into thinking that from now on it *must* be all right. He then leaves the sphere of AT and falls back into the area of ambivalence between hope and disappointment—and thus also into the autoaggressive behavior patterns of the imperative "must," when confronted with the obvious fact of his inability or partial ability.

A basketful of intentional formulae. Let us keep to the above example and follow developments. At the point where the amazed discovery of effortless speaking turns all the stutterer's previous experience on its head, the formula used until now, "breath carries the words," is no longer sufficient. This formula does not encompass the whole syndrome of inhibition stuttering—especially as its causes differ from one patient to another, and the combination of factors differs according to personality—quantitatively, qualitatively, and also as regards predominance. Even before he has reached this critical juncture, the patient, under the guidance of the instructor, can be brought to analyze the position that has been reached with the help of this formula. By himself, or better with the assistance of his instructor, the stutterer accepts that, in spite of the generally constructive effect of the formula, "slips" still occur if particular letters or whole words have to be pronounced which somehow seem to tie up with his inhibition. Now, in the example we are following, the addition of a further formula could pave the way to more fluent speech. "Addressing people goes smoothly too" or "breath can even carry . . ." (insert the word most closely linked with the inhibition). The trainee can, after a while, draw on a few intentional formulae which he may use alternately or in combination. In this store of intentional formulae, he has a repertoire of which he himself is in charge; together with the instructor, he controls its composition and the apropriateness of its individual elements.

The best-known intentional formulae are those for giving up drinking or smoking. Those formulae that trivialize the problem and do not pay due account to the importance of

these habits will not suffice. Anyone who cannot stop drinking or smoking is—however you may wish to understand the
word—dependent in a way which deserves to be taken
seriously. "Smoking doesn't matter," a much-praised formula, might be effective in some cases. In those cases where
it does help, smoking was not a deeply ingrained habit; it
didn't "count." A categorically negative formula with strong
powers of suggestion must be worked out by the smoker or
drinker with the instructor if the habit really is to be broken.

A word of caution. The task in hand can be coped with only
if the necessary trance state is permanently at the subject's
disposal—something he can call on at any time. Those need-
ing treatment for drinking and smoking problems will only
very rarely have the persistence to master AT within three or
four months. The most popular form of treatment is hypnosis. The heterosuggestive basis established by means of a
deep or moderate trance is open to posthypnotic suggestions
of the necessary strength and quality. The continuation and
further reinforcing of the abstinence can be managed extremely well with AT, which is then learned with suitable intentional formulae. Depending on the personality of the subject and his attitude to his addiction problem, the required
prohibition formula can incorporate explicit warning phrases
which draw his attention to the consequences of his habit.
The doctor must be able to judge to what extent he may justi-
fiably fixate the patient, by means of posthypnotic suggestions and intentional formulae, on his existential fears, especially with regard to his responsibilities toward his family.

Not everyone who wants to break the smoking or drinking

habit, which he sees as a blot on his self-image, is an addict or an alcoholic. On the whole, the majority are merely people who are inclined that way or who have weaknesses which they cannot accept as part of themselves. Thus one can count nibbling along with smoking and drinking, and also unbridled pleasurable eating which is then followed by feelings of guilt. It is significant that, among those people who react ambivalently to the struggle between pleasure and subsequent discomfort, some come to the clinic with a masturbation problem, because subjectively they see the problem as an addiction, as a "not being able to stop," whereas this problem is objectively much further removed from addiction and has quite different psychological determinants.

With an adequate number of intentional formulae—as few as possible but as many as are needed—more serious disturbances of concentration and of psycho-physical effectiveness can be treated. Concentrative relaxation is a descriptive definition of AT. Trainees find that, in the routine recapitulation of the basic formulae once they have mastered them, most concentration problems dissolve. A prime example from daily life is supplied by candidates for examinations in all fields. The standard formulae and intentional formulae on the lines of "the exam proves that I have worked" free the candidate from the pressure to achieve which he has developed either spontaneously from his own ideals, or in response to the influence of others and to uncritical comparisons.

Experience teaches us that intentional formulae lose their edge and "wear out" more quickly than the standard formulae of the basic training, which express collectively human states of physical being and are thus able to remain ineradica-

bly present. Therefore a whole sheaf of formulae is to be recommended for work on character-related behavior patterns
that need correcting. The experienced and still practicing
trainee calls on this supply for possibilities of improving his
condition. Popular offers in the style of pamphlets like "How
to Be Energetic" or "The Way to Success" can now be seen
from the right perspective. A person in a state of psycho-
physical harmony, in a critical equilibrium between desire
and ability, will find that what is appropriate for him succeeds spontaneously, autogenically (from within), and also
autotropically (with reference to his own self). Such a person
has learned and continues to learn, through practice, just
what his possibilities and limitations are.

As the practiced art of a relaxed letting-be, AT is also in
its essence a school of tolerance. To the oft-quoted words of
Schultz, "only he who lets himself be can be himself," we
can add "he who tolerates himself is tolerant."

Independent verbalization *ad lib*

In the course of his training, the trainee has been encouraged
to construct his own intentional formulae according to need.
During this time he has had the chance to scrutinize his
formulations with his instructor and to polish them. One
should keep up AT all one's life. There is no intelligent
reason not to, unless of course the instruction was mediocre,
the motivation weak, and the whole course geared with unnecessary rigidity to one solitary symptom. But no one remains fixated on his AT instructor all his life. In any case,
with respect for the autonomy of the personality, it is not
desirable for the teacher-pupil relationship to be prolonged.

The less detail is laid down in the oral or written instruction, the greater the latitude that the trainee has both during the course and afterwards, when he finds himself confronted with the question: "A new problem, a disturbance—what do I do about that autogenically?"

The need to take up AT again after the passage of time is only to be expected. No matter what the original reason was for learning AT, new reasons will come up in the course of one's further life. This should be mentioned as part of the instruction. Ever since my own experience of individual patients who came back years later, unable to cope with a new situation and without having had the idea of applying AT to it on their own, I have incorporated this into the basic training.

First, regenerate the standard formulae. All abilities fall into disuse; even AT can become completely silted up—but it can never be forgotten. Anyone who has any reason to freshen up his AT, which he has not been practicing regularly and which has perhaps degenerated, should spend one or two weeks on a concentrated relearning of all the standard formulae. Even if, in a state of relaxation, individual "basic stage" experiences stand out like islands, the regeneration of the training should proceed systematically and it should be recalled step by step. Spontaneous organic experiences, generalization, and other still-retained bits of the training can be incorporated. At the end of the second week at the latest, with relaxed but regular repetition, the whole of AT should once again be at one's fingertips.

The buried talent. Intentional formulae that were of good use earlier and which might be applicable to the new situation form the matrix for further work beyond the basic stage. Very valuable in this respect are the organ formulae which improve unsatisfactory responses in the autogenic shift. Playing around with combinations of formulae for mutual intensification, as described earlier in this book, completes the refresher course in AT.

New situation—new formula. In a new situation the former instructor, should he be available, can help. But how does the proficient trainee help himself when he is alone and has no one to turn to? Summarized below are a few basic recommendations which will enable the more experienced to construct their own formulae independently, as the need arises:

The basic form simple statement	A simple statement modeled on the formulae of the basic training achieves the following goal: the complaint is approached positively, one's interest in it is expressed positively and has no overtones—neither offensive, with an eye to eradicating it, nor defensive, with an eye to repressing it. Model: "pulse calm and regular."
content apodictically certain	The intentional formula must be true as far as its content goes. Facts are looked honestly in the eye. The situation is seen mercilessly pointblank but with

absolute tolerance. Model: "My desk is chaotic."

tense and mood
present indicative

Every intentional formula must be in the present indicative. In AT nothing "becomes"; it "is." The future tense means postponement, the present allows one to experience the actual.

negation
if in doubt, no

Negation goes deep and hits the ego at its most vulnerable point. Categorical negations can be justified as particular exceptions. The autodidact can easily run into danger. The affirmative, confirmatory form of speech is basically a reassurance of the ego. Even formulae which have the intention of removing a disturbing factor can, with a little skill, be formulated positively.

imperative—the voice of the superego
allow it; do not force it

The intentional formula is not a "good intention" in the morally imperative mode. It is rather the formulation of an intention (which can take root in the trance state), the idea of that which, seen functionally, would be right in the place of what has previously been wrong. Thus: not want, should, must; but expect, allow.

memorability
by heart

Brevity and succinctness together with the rhythm of the intentional formula make it a piece of oneself. To recognize oneself in the formula means to be concerned with oneself in the functional disturbance and to visualize the desired normal functioning as attainable; the rejected aspects of one's personality structure are to be judged realistically, and realizable concepts of the self are to be entertained. Model: "I see myself."

testing stage
the courage to reformulate

There is no point in clinging to a formula if it does not "work." Filing and polishing on the formula is not always enough. Sometimes matters improve only when a completely new formula is introduced.

complex formulae
narrowing the focus

The somatic disturbance being dealt with, the desired behavioral change can sometimes elude a direct approach by means of intentional formulae. In such cases it is necessary to proceed step by step, narrowing things down and at the same time becoming increasingly stringent.

Examples:

"pulse calm and regular" (in basic training)

"pulse regular in public speaking too"

"pulse regular in discussion"

"pulse always regular"

and

"redheads are human too"

"I observe redheads, I notice them"

"Erica has red hair"

"Erica's hair is her hair"

a reflexive formula

AT as intentional formula

Those who have chronic difficulties in persevering with AT and do not want to become lax about it should ideally make use of:

"My AT"

"AT good—I'm sticking with it"

Notes on intentional formulae

"With the concept 'speech doesn't matter' I am almost always overcome by the feeling that I shall manage everything effortlessly and that formerly I used to get much too upset."

"With the formula 'I know who I am' the feeling of rest grows stronger and things harmonize. I have a stronger feeling of security."

"Pulse and heaviness immediately. Warmth at the appropriate exercise. At every formula I now speak inwardly while breathing out. Pulse is concentrated the whole time mainly on the diaphragm. Plexus formula going well. Intentional formula: 'I speak with the flow.' At once a much greater expulsion of breath. The intervals between breathing in and out become correspondingly greater. With this, waves of warmth through my whole body."

" 'Courage and self-confidence are increasing.' 'I am calm in every activity.' Relaxation particularly good with these personal formulae, which I fit in between the standard formulae."

"I got up today and went to the kindergarten without any feelings of anxiety or nervousness. I've been practicing splendidly with the formula 'this is my working day.' "

Consecutive notes

These notes were made by a twenty-five-year-old teacher, who suffered from sexual anxiety and from physical aversion to her fiancé, who was fat. The notes were taken over a four-month period, from September to January. From February to April inclusive, the patient gives two separate summaries of the results of her practice sessions—sitting, and lying down.

9/12   Stifled feeling. Cramped inward listening. Pounding of the belly artery. Then a feeling of warmth, rising from the fingertips to the elbow.

9/13   No inner peace—pressure in head and throat.

9/14 Pulsating body, pounding in the right thigh—body heavy.

9/15 Belly wall drawn downwards. Droning in head.

9/16 Warmth rising from the toes to the knees.

9/17 Pounding in head and warmth rising from the feet to the knees and from the fingertips to the elbows. Feeling as if I were turning.

9/21 Yesterday's good mood lets me find inner peace. [Note: patient visited her fiancé.] Cardiac twinges, numbness in head—tickling in the hands, warmth rising in my back.

9/22 No real concentration. Pressure in the throat. A sort of strangled feeling.

9/24 The right side of the upper part of the body is heavier than the left. Right arm is heavy. Rushing sound. Left arm doesn't exist. Tickling on the back of hands, moves into the forearm and up to the elbow.

9/25 No physical equilibrium.

9/28 Hunger makes my belly wall contract. Tickling feelings in both arms. I have the feeling in my right arm: the cold arm is slowly warming up. At the same time it is as heavy as lead.

9/30 I am aware of the length of my legs. I can feel the whole extent of my body. Tickling feelings in the right arm.

10/1 Feel the extent of my body; right arm and right leg heavy as lead.

10/2 Again this feeling of the surface of my body.

10/5 Right arm almost without feeling. Warmth spreads through the whole body.

10/8 Heaviness in the right arm quickly achieved. Warmth creeps into arms and legs and then throughout body. Light arm causes feeling of weightlessness.

10/9   Right arm heavy and warm. Body heavy as lead.

10/10   Through "breath calm and regular" the opposite, gasping for breath.

10/12   Concentration quickly achieved. Breath goes better without the formula.

10/13   Faltering breath. All parts of the body that are touching the couch are warm.

10/15   Paralyzing tickling in both arms. Back of my head, touching the couch, is painfully heavy. [Note: patient discovered that she had some awkwardly positioned hairpins in her bun.]

10/17   Body quickly warm.

10/19   Regular, calm breath, rhythmical pulsation on the surface of the body.

10/20   Warmth comes immediately after lying down.

10/21   Floating feeling in both feet.

10/22   Rhythmical pulsation in face and hands.

10/23   Feeling that my hands are floating.

10/24   A delightful feeling of warmth fills my whole body.

10/25   Body quickly warm.

10/26   Calm breath. Muscles relax. Body becomes heavy.

10/27   Rhythmical pulsation in my face, then on the backs of the hands, then in the arms.

10/28   Warmth comes promptly.

10/29   Overslept my usual session. At lunch break tried to make up for it but found no inner peace.

11/2   Warm body. Muscles limp. Body heavy as lead. Feeling as if my right hand were swollen.

11/4   Warmth comes promptly. Blockage of warmth in knees. Tickling in head. Skin of forehead tense.

11/5   Arms and head warm, feet cold, body pulsating.

11/6   Warm, heavy, pulsating body.

11/8   Pulsating body, icy cold hands get warm during the session.

11/9 Warm body, cold hands get warmer. A tingling in my whole body.

11/11 Stomach rumbling. Belly artery pulsating. Belly wall presses. [Note: the patient means here a pressing of the belly wall on the intestines.]

11/12 Stomach gurgling. Belly enclosed in the warmth of the body.

11/13 Warm body. Belly wall falls into belly. Belly artery pulsates. Feeling of warmth extends to the whole abdomen.

11/14 Belly wall is heavy—gets gradually lighter. Belly artery pulsates. Warmth focuses on the sex organs.

11/16 Warm body, cool forehead, pulsating abdomen; clothes, stockings, etc., no longer exist; I am surrounded by a warm skin.

11/18 Beating, relaxed abdomen, cool forehead, tingling body. For the first time practiced intentional formula: "Fat people are attractive too." [Note: the patient chose this formula herself and it was given to her to try out.]

11/21 Warm heavy body; pulsing belly artery. Intentional formula: "Plump cheeks don't bother me."

11/23 Belly wall tense, pulsating belly artery. Heavy body.

11/25 Heavy, tired body, warm abdomen. Intentional formula.

11/28 Pulsing of the aorta. "Fat people are attractive too, plump cheeks don't bother me."

12/1 Cold hands warm up. Tingling arms, pulsing aorta, relaxed belly wall.

12/4 Warm body, relaxed belly wall. Intentional formula: "Face pleasing."

[Note: The patient practiced less along these lines over Christmas, and then again very regularly in January, and made notes much like the above. On January 20 she noted: "warm body, scrape on leg, painful during circulation; relaxed belly wall."]

1/23 Tingling body. New intentional formula: "Eric's fatness is irrelevant, the body widens."

[Note: For the months from February to April, inclusive, the patient gives two separate summaries for practice sessions sitting and lying down.]

Lying: Feet and hands, especially the palms, get warm quickly. Warmth rises up to the shoulders. Warmth concentrated on the knees and shoulder blades. Hiccoughs disappear. Head attains very marked heaviness. I continue to practice with various intentional formulae, sometimes, "Eric is like that"; other times, "Eric is good, his appearance is part of him." With this training I can reach complete relaxation.

Sitting: Cramped sitting position, cramped posture, tense neck. Aches in back and neck. Hands and feet get warm. Back and neck become less tense, I notice this especially during evening sessions. Training in this position is easier. Hands, feet, whole body becomes warm. Tingling feeling in hands, feet, and legs. Heavy head falls forwards. Training in this position does not lead to complete relaxation, but it does go more quickly. Concentration does not last so long because of the accompanying physical symptoms.

[Note: One further last summarizing note for the months May to July.]

Warmth creeps throughout my body, clearly observable in the toes and fingertips. Arms, hands and feet "expand." Body is heavy as lead, especially the calves. All parts that touch the couch form a unity with it. Feet no longer feel the presence of my shoes. Organs in the belly are heavy. Pulsation in head and body which then diminishes. Palms begin to tingle even before I begin the session. Lately I can do AT even in the company of quiet people. Final intentional formula, in which I focus directly on my fiancé: ''Eric is fine, just as he is.''

V

THE ADVANCED STAGE

In an early publication, J. H. Schultz gives an introductory survey of the possibilities of a further differentiation of AT, and indicates in what directions these differentiations lead.[1] After speaking of the psychical representation of organic experiences, such as I have described in this detailed presentation of the basic training, drawn from the experience of both the author and of his whole school, Schultz discusses the discovery of the particular "animation of the body." By this he means not so much the mere appropriation to self-awareness of otherwise autonomous physical control mechanisms, but rather he acknowledges that the trainee is able to deepen the experience of physical identity. Further, Schultz interprets the ability of the trainee to create external sensory experiences by means of intensive self-absorption. Here he means

---

1. J. H. Schultz, "Gehobene Aufgabenstufen im AT" ("Applications of AT at more advanced levels") contained in the Report on the Proceedings of the IVth General Medical Congress for Psychotherapy, Bad Nauheim, April 1929. Reprinted in *Der Weg des Autogene Training* (page 73 ff.), Wissenschaftlich Buchgesellschaft, Darmstadt.

the interiorizing of external experiences with the effect of their being more deeply anchored in the experiential capital of the person. Even habitual actions are more deeply ingrained and integrated: in this way they become "personal property." Finally, the author presents heightened self-contemplation as the highest level of differentiated AT.

A further point of this particular work is concerned with the autonomy of the interior structure. In this state of absorption—deconcentrated, focusing on the interior experiences without distraction and turning more and more to the dreamlike depths—the subject increasingly manifests his essential self in the nature of his experiences. The form and organization of the material that is presented—its richness, liveliness and luxuriance on the one hand and on the other aridity and poverty; colorful concrete manifestations in all areas of sense-perception, or schematic, abstract reactions; a confusion of petty detail, or a stark structure; chaos or rhythm; tending backwards or forwards—all these characteristics indicate apparently typologically elementary phenomena and are here able to develop and reveal themselves.[2]

In this connection Schultz arrives at the concept of autopsychocatharsis, a sort of autopsychoanalysis which can reach astounding depths. Although in this particular work the term "advanced stage" does not appear, it is clear that the origins of this technique are as plainly indicated here as previously the particular potential of the intentional formulae.

In his AT teaching manual, Schultz introduced his chapter on "The Technique and Achievements of the Advanced Stage" with sentences of such importance that I would like to quote them verbatim:

---

2. Ibid., p. 82

To reach the advanced level in our technique it is a prerequisite that there be a sure, complete and prompt mastery of the general technique of the basic training. Trainees must be able, by means of very brief acts of inner concentration, to bring about the specific shift immediately so that the body is experienced as a heavy, warm, resting mass with regular pulse and tranquil breath, somehow separate from the cool, deconcentrated head. This state is so remarkable and so characteristic that trainees who have had no contact with each other remarkably often find the identical words to describe it.[3]

I devise my advanced courses starting from the same basis, whether I am dealing with individuals or groups, and make use of the spontaneous anticipatory experience of the trainees. It is just as true for the advanced level as it was for the basic course that autonomously determined inner experiences of the trainees assert themselves and—often in anticipation of the course material—give rise to unplanned instruction. Some people think that, in AT, to say anything that is not directly connected with what is being taught is either wrong or irrelevant. Thus such utterances are mostly either kept to oneself or they lead to anxious questioning of the instructor. Only through the keeping of regular notes, which I have always insisted upon, have body experiences that have taken place even in the basic training come to light.

More rare are reports of color experiences, which most trainees seem to find distracting and which are for this reason repressed. Thomas estimates that about two to three percent of trainees report such color experiences unprompted. When notes are insisted upon, the percentage increases somewhat,

---

3. J. H. Schultz, *Das Autogenes Training*, Thieme-Verlag, Stuttgart 1970, p. 228.

and my own most recent experiences have led me to differentiate in the interpretation of thought content and purely visual imaginings even in the early sessions of a course. Thoughts that are merely distracting should by all means be pushed aside, but the visual experiences should be accepted neutrally and carried along during the exercise.

Work on the advanced stage of AT is, then, a spontaneous meditative absorption on the basis of the trance achieved in the basic training. In the case of all spontaneous experiences that tend to have this quality, it is an undirected and unsought absorption which we cannot value highly enough as an anticipation on the part of the trainee. Before coming to speak of the technique of the advanced exercises, some ideas about meditation in general and the relationship between advanced-level meditation and other psycho-physical matters should be clarified.

General remarks about meditation

The word comes from Latin. *Meditari* means to reflect; meditation is a reflection on something, a thoughtful contemplation. It does not mean a concentrated thinking about something. Meditation is essentially a collecting, a gathering-in, whereas thinking, cogitation, is a sending-out of thoughts in prescribed directions. The opposite and contradictory natures of the two should thus be clear.

Meditation as a collecting always needs a certain amount of physical reinforcement. All meditative techniques and situations have one thing in common: they establish a specific preparatory posture which induces and supports the course of the meditation. The meditative postures of the Far East are generally known, especially the meditative sitting position (the lotus position). The meditation of prayer, too, uses the more or less standardized postures of the standing, kneeling, or prostrate worshipper. The meditative techniques of the advanced stage of AT follow from the already obtaining relaxation of the basic stage and have no need of a further posture. Externally, therefore, one cannot tell from the appearance of a trainee how far he has advanced in his exercises.

Meditation is a reflecting on a particular content, whether we are thinking of philosophical, religious, or other psychophysical meditations of profound absorption. The contents are determined by the expectations of the person embarking upon meditation. All absorbed contemplations of visualized objects should be reckoned as meditative exercises, among them the inner relationship to spiritual contents, especially those mystically religious or generally ethical in nature. There is a great deal of relevant literature about meditation in general and its countless individual forms. Many people, in the course of their lives, have been introduced to certain habits of meditation, either through their own interest, through education, or through contact with other people. Not a few of them have thereby found a great enrichment of their own inner lives.

The advanced stage as self-contemplation

If Schultz, in the early work of 1929 from which I have quoted, indicated self-contemplation as the third and highest of the differentiated further developments of AT, it remained to his pupils, right up to the present day, to work this out methodically. In the space available to me here, I will present the advanced stage as an intensification of the capacity for experience and the ability to direct the images that arise.

Advanced autogenic training, under proper guidance, literally opens windows through which perceptions crowd in—for the most part completely new, and qualitatively either positive or negative. Autodidactic attempts at advanced AT on the basis of the available literature can be even more problematical than the attempt to master the basic training on one's own. Unaided first attempts at experiences proper to the advanced stage either lead to fatigue and the dissipation of the experience accompanied by a growing resistance to the occurrence of images, or the autodidact becomes confused and worried by the profusion and incomprehensibility of the images. The task of the instructor in the advanced stage is a very responsible one and is essentially more delicate than in the basic training, since the formulae for the advanced stage, as well as the organization and procedure of the advanced sessions, are less standardized. The individuality of every participant in an advanced course needs much more support and care than was the case in the comparatively clear-cut basic stage.

The first experiences in the advanced stage strike the trainee as vague, unclear, and sometimes upsetting. Even if the experiences themselves are pleasant, they are at first alien and puzzling. Development in the advanced stage is not nearly so straightforward as in the basic stage. The danger is much greater that some participants in the course, the less proficient, will come to see themselves as failures in comparison with others who present their own more highly differentiated experiences for general discussion. The continually repeated support for all participants focuses mainly on the confirmation that every image produced in the advanced training is important in itself and cannot be measured, qualitatively or quantitatively, against any evaluative norm.

What does the trainee see in the advanced course? According to the directions given, but not necessarily following any given instructions—that is, allowing for anticipation as well as for catching up—he sees colors, shapes, landscapes, actions, persons, and perhaps himself. These inner experiences of self-contemplation cannot be arranged according to any schemata but must be seen in their relationship to the person experiencing them. Note-taking thus becomes even more important and is comparable with making notes of dreams or writing down thoughts in a diary or a letter. The general discussion during the course, carefully steered by the instructor, or the psychotherapeutic discussion in individual instruction calls for a purposeful, careful, and responsible presentation of any attitudes or reactions by the instructor that either immediately take up or freely interpret what has been offered by the trainee at that moment, and in either case they should not go beyond it. The individual self-contemplation of the trainees defines the limits of what the instructor may or may not take up—both in content and in terms of the further possibilities for association. Hence the first commandment for both instructor and trainees is the greatest possible respect for any self-revelations either in spontaneous imagery or in advanced AT meditation.

In a well-conducted course this only rarely causes difficulty. The inner solidarity and the common goal of those taking part create an atmosphere of mutual respect, unquestioning awareness, and appreciation. The advanced course, usually numbering ten to at most fifteen participants, creates an atmosphere of intimacy and fellowship among those bound together in an undertaking, the innate privacy of which demands tactful discretion within the group.

Advanced training in a group is teamwork in the true sense of the word. Mutual support is the motive for the sensitive communication that takes place. The usual quickness of action and reaction that one otherwise meets in psychotherapeutically oriented groups, particularly in verbal encounter groups, is minimal in advanced AT groups. The training session and the subsequent group reporting and questioning arises out of a state of freshly experienced deep contemplation in a condition of complete physical and psychical relaxation. Hence the aggressive potential found in most types of group therapy is lacking. The presence of the instructor, himself a master of the method, guarantees the unity of the group and also a high degree of critical self-revelation. As soon as a trainee, his own inner goal achieved, has "returned" from his training, he remains awhile in the afterglow of the experience and observes the others, some of them still in their training, others like himself sitting or lying in quiet reflection. Only when all have "returned" do the unprompted individual communications occur. Being silent and retaining one's experience for oneself, should any have such a need, should be accepted both by the instructor and by the other participants.

The self-contemplation of trainees in the advanced course

arises out of the organismic shift and may be restricted to a few solitary color experiences or other simple representations of the inner vision. Others have more dynamic, more varied experiences. Once again, we must remember that in the advanced level it is not a question of particular quantities or qualities of experience, but solely of the individual in the here and now. Thus the self-reflective state that ensues is only partially communicable. If a participant wishes to communicate, he offers his own interior experiences to the others present. Similarly, each takes part in the presentation of other forms and other contents of self-contemplation, not infrequently with an obvious empathy and sympathetic agreement with what has been uttered.

Self-contemplation in the advanced stage means recognition of one's own depths. Communication of one's own self-contemplation, and receptivity toward what others reveal as their experiences of themselves, leads to a fundamental group experience which, by its nature and especially at the advanced level, has the effect of intensification within the group. Here too a general group law is valid: the individual experiences himself in the group through the group itself. What is therapeutically special here is the combination of group intensification with the greatest possible group cohesion. Advanced training in groups is thus group therapy of a very special sort.

Individual instruction at the advanced level must do without such group intensification. But to make up for that, it gains, through the one-to-one relationship of therapist and patient or trainee, an enrichment of understanding through more intensive interpretative work and more richly varied exploration of associations. Advanced-level AT has long been valued by those who know and have mastered it as a therapeutic technique of depth psychology. It ranks as a much shortened depth-psychological therapy compared with the greater investment of time which conventional psychoanalysis demands. And with this observation, no value judgments are intended with regard to the effectivity of any given method in any individual case.

Advanced level, free association, and dream

The advanced level of AT is, then, a meditative practice of a particular sort. Its most important feature is that, according to my own understanding of its original premise, its use is not linked to any particular ends and that—apart from having an ordered structure moving from the simple to the complex—it gives no direct instructions to the meditating individual. In contrast to other hypnotic techniques, it merely enables the trainee to open himself to images that arise spontaneously.

I think this introduction has been necessary. As will be shown in the next section, which deals with techniques, many doctors and instructors work with the advanced training without taking this basic premise into account, whereby in my view they reduce the advanced level quite clearly to a heterogenic technique. Here again I can only fall back on the teachings of Schultz, which he insisted upon right through to the last edition of his teaching manual. He has the following to say concerning the basic concept of the advanced level:

> Just as with experiences of night-dream, in a good example of autogenic contemplation—and I have often stressed this—

the psychological constitution of the subject is relaxed to such a degree that, apart from a few exceptional cases, we can always reach the stage of optical experiences, a literal "looking within," experience in pictures. W. Luthe has made a special study of visual experiences in the autogenic state.[4] He distinguishes color motifs, shapes, and dynamic motifs which sometimes tend more toward reality, sometimes toward the unreal world, and is quite right in stressing the importance of a *carte blanche* attitude if a person does wish to look within— the importance of his being completely unprejudiced. This phenomenon is, one might say, our raw material. At the beginning of the advanced-level course, we give the following first assignment: we ask the subject, while he is in a state of deep absorption, to let a field of any one color appear before his inner eye. This and his subsequent efforts demand that he remain in this state of absorption for half an hour to an hour. This is something which one can ask only of trainees if they have been doing AT regularly for at least six months, and preferably for a whole year or more, and are at home, as it were, in the state of absorption. Even this first exercise, the evoking of a field of any uniform, homogeneous color, can tell us many interesting things. In the terms of our technique, we speak of the discovery of one's own color.[5]

The raw material referred to here, vivid images, primarily visual, must remind anyone who has had contact with such things, either in his own personal experience or through his patients if he is a psychoanalyst, of the visual representations that are produced in dreams and free association. The images that arise in the advanced level are immanent; they are memories and thus the personal property of the trainee. They arise from the unconscious and present themselves as fragments.

4. *Correlationes Psychosomaticae*, 1965, p. 171.
5. Schultz, *Lehrbuch*, p. 231.

The direct parallel between advanced-level dream images and free association has, of course, been noticed by many advanced-level instructors. Thus it is all the more astonishing that a cautious approach, modeled on that of analytical associative and interpretative work, does not prevail, and that strictly prescribed practicing of a set course of exercises in the advanced level is what sometimes takes place.

W. Luthe wrote about this in the summary of an article: "The fragmentary and primitive visionary phenomena which occur during conventional basic AT exercises tend to a greater differentiation and to logical sequences in those cases where the trainee, well versed in AT, performs a mental shift of function from the formula-oriented passive concentration to a formula-free passive acceptance (*carte blanche*). The therapist, in keeping with the basic premises of AT, maintains a respectful, noninterfering attitude toward the products of the mental mechanisms of the patient." [6] Here we have, in the words of a strictly scientifically-minded researcher among pioneers of AT, a clear rejection of a relapsing into heterosuggestion and heterohypnosis. Equally pointed is the rejection expressed at the congress *"Arzt und Seelsorger"* (Doctor and Pastor) at Schloss Elmau in 1972 by another pupil of the first generation, Schaetzing, who stated: "The whole of AT is and remains a purely medical concern, and is thus our concern; whereas the standard training has a mainly somatopsychic application, in the advanced level, psychosomatic self-knowledge blossoms forth which can be spoken of in the same breath as the results of psychoanalysis."

---

6. *Correlationes Psychosomaticae*, 1965, p. 189.

To sum up my own opinions, drawing on my own experiences, both personally and through my patients and trainees: I have long been aware that the images of the advanced level arise from the same depths of the subject's unconscious as the contents of dreams and the free associations these give rise to in psychoanalytic treatment. But it is useful to distinguish between them, and it deepens one's understanding of their relationship to do so. All the notes from advanced courses that I have at my disposal establish that the images from advanced AT are clearer, more vividly colored, and in general more lasting than dream images, even than those of particularly impressive dreams which one remembers for life. The advanced-level images come unbidden, stay, change, give way suddenly to new, totally different images, and disappear as they came. They cannot be deliberately called back; but by a deliberate act of memory they can be recalled.

This raw material is indeed a harvest of immeasurable wealth for those who eventually associate further from this basis and then fuse these images both with each other and with the free associations and dreams of the same period into one complex of meaning, or one externalization of their inner life.

The products of daydreams must be strictly distinguished from those of the advanced level—and here, too, the parallel dream/daydream is evident. In daydreams, the wool-gathering person produces "favorite" images, usually of an ego-reinforcing nature, and thus not freely but very much bound to associations. In contrast, the images of the advanced level, dreams, and free associations are only in part at the service of a regressive, illusionary self-aggrandizement. The majority of these latter images spring from unconscious levels, often fear-ridden, often in baffling disguise, and always with a "poetic" compression of content that is concentrated where the axes of the various determinants intersect. To unravel this calls for systematic analytical work, even within the limits of the advanced course. Any further instruction and practice of the advanced level must, however, be a matter for an actual AT course and cannot be dealt with within the confines of this book.

The method

The methodical procedure in advanced-level work has been presented, with many elucidative examples, in the relevant chapter of Schultz's instruction manual. Briefly, there are five steps:

1. The experience of color. The finding of a color and the development of this exercise to the discovery and retention of the so called "personal color." The goal is a mastery of these initial color experiences—an ability to repeat this experience at will.

2. The assignment is to have particular objects appear before one's inner eye. "Here the subject frequently leaves the realm of the allegorical and crosses to that of the symbolic. He experiences these images three-dimensionally. He can walk around them and is himself overwhelmed by the unusualness and the wealth of his experiences. And it is here that our work, strictly speaking, begins to be productive, as many subjects are not only showered with beautiful inner experiences but also enriched for their further lives." [7]

---

7. Schultz, *Lehrbuch*, p. 240.

3. The trainee seeks, for his self-contemplation, some experience or other that is the expression or the epitome of the most intense and most desired emotional state. (Schultz suggests, analogous to the first exercise with the "personal color," that we here speak of the "personal feeling.")

4. After this experience of one's inner life, the next assignment is, in a state of deep absorption, to visualize quite concretely a particular other person, and to let oneself react to this.

5. Questioning attitudes are directed to the absorbed state itself and the inner experiences that arise, as answers from the unconscious, are noted down.

With regard to this fifth exercise, Schultz remarks that this technique can be used either by the instructor or by the trainee himself. I wish to draw attention to this because, although I am strictly opposed to any heterogenic subversion of AT, in the case of this fifth exercise I myself like to see the lead taken by the instructor, with the proviso that this must be in the form of half-questioning, half-deliberating invitations on the part of the instructor which are free of any suggestive bias.

Luthe speaks of the structure of the advanced stage as having seven steps. In his presentation, the actual external differences are only slight but the inner development is treated more concretely:

> Seven phases can be distinguished with regard to visionary phenomena with a range from the simple to highly complex configurations which may or may not be derived from experiences:
> 1. static uniform colors
> 2. dynamic polymorphic colors

3. color patterns and simple shapes
4. unmoving objects
5. the transformation of objects and the progressive differentiation of images
6. increased continuity of images with participation of the subject (film-strip)
7. cinerama effect with emotional participation of the subject.[8]

Luthe's interpretation of the processes of the advanced stage, which is strongly oriented towards neurophysiology, provides an interesting approach from a second point of view as well, and one which does not really conflict with the teachings of Schultz or with my own presentation.

Klaus Thomas, an early pupil of Schultz's, conducts a course of seven two-hour periods for the advanced stage. Up to the fourth step he follows essentially the structure of his teacher. But even as early as the experience of color, he formulates the instructions in such a strongly heterosuggestive way that one quotation will serve to illustrate his unorthodox interpretation and teaching of the advanced stage: "A color develops in front of my eyes; it is my personal color." He has these words repeated about five times, and follows up with: "The color is getting clearer and clearer." Finally comes the instruction: "I can see the color quite plainly."

It is beyond doubt that by this means, color experiences can be produced with great rapidity in the majority of trainees. It remains to be asked whether this result is in fact autogenic and whether it has, as its content, the things that the trainee is really concerned with during the exercise. Thomas

---

8. *Correlationes Psychosomaticae*, p. 189.

also allows the color to fade gradually by means of similar formulae, and to disappear on suggestion.

The fifth two-hour period in Thomas's course is called "the way to the bottom of the sea." Here Thomas is drawing on the experiments and experiences of Berta (Montevideo), Desoille, and Leuner. The idea of sending the trainee, suggestively, to the bottom of the sea has its source in an underlying notion of giving him a vertical concept of direction. Thomas himself writes: "The patient is instructed, without further [*sic!*] influence, to betake himself downwards—to the depths of the sea—and later upwards—to the top of a high mountain." [9] The way to the mountain peak, the sixth period, is thus defined as the contrary vertical direction. The seventh period is used for free and guided image-experiences with specific goals.

My own dislike of giving trainees and patients unnecessary guidance instruction makes it impossible for me to work along the lines of Thomas's method. I teach the advanced stage according to Luthe, as I find his method convincing in its logical structure. It allows me to integrate the experiences reported to me in private instruction and in group courses into the scheme of the course, as if into a diagram. Didactically, I proceed much like Schultz. In my fifteen years of experience with AT, mainly in intensive individual instruction, I have carried over the free-floating alertness that I maintain in my work as an analytical psychotherapist to my procedure in AT courses. I have come to the following realizations:

The trainee in the advanced stage usually first produces

9. *Praxis der Selbsthypnose*, p. 57.

discrepant and often discordant individual images, and hesitates for a time in the choice between individual colors. Notes indicate that, in time, one color begins to predominate. Only when this has happened do I introduce the expression "personal color." Once this stage has been reached in the cooperative interpretation of the color experiences so far, it is in some cases possible to attempt, very cautiously, some verbal interpretation, or at least to ask a few questions. At the point at which the trainee ceases to react with attentiveness, dismay, or a visible "aha!" I break off the questions. Of course, at this stage, the trainee normally has already had experiences—quite spontaneously—of static shapes and sometimes even of dynamic, moving objects. He will then, without a rigid scheme of exercises, be directed toward a contemplation of these advanced-level images. At this stage I lay great value on a differentiation, which my own experience demands, between unmistakably genuine advanced-level images and those images remembered from recent experiences, which can occur along with them. It strikes me as important to draw a line between spontaneous, freely arising, advanced-level images and mere memories. The latter are usually an indication that the trainee is rising to the surface of his state of absorption and has begun to incorporate fragments from his daily life into his images. I encourage my trainees at this point to return to the basic training and to deepen their trance. The day's odds and ends and memories that have cropped up are, for the rest, not given any further attention, neither as regards content nor in general, and I avoid letting them appear to have been a "mistake" or failure. To those trainees who would respond to the interpretation, I present these fragmentary memories of real experiences as similar to the tag-ends of our night dreams that we remember during the day. Any other interpretation must come from the trainee himself, and from him alone. Then I take up whatever it is that he presents. Such digressions do not disturb the course of the training-discussion in the least. We are aware that we have temporarily gone off on a tangent, and then we return to a consideration of the advanced-level material proper.

The experiences of the advanced level, increasingly more vivid and more dynamic, offer in the course of the advanced training a wealth of opportunity for interpretation in depth. And since I have reached this point with all of my trainees, I have never seen any necessity to send them to the mountain peak or to the bottom of the sea. Experiences of vertical dimension occur in various guises without prompting; they are neither didactically planned, nor do they need to be called by name in the interpretation. On the contrary, the trainee who has had such experiences of being abandoned in the depths, or of the laborious and liberating path to the mountaintop has such a multitude of related associations as cannot all be gone into, and which perhaps do not need to be interpreted fully.

In individual instructions I arrange my timetable according to the amount of material available. It is not the daily routine, which is so indispensable in the basic training, that needs to be controlled in the sessions, but the advanced-level exercises, which are linked with a great deal of basic-level work. Even those who practice regularly do advanced-level work on their own only sporadically. As soon as they want to proceed further, we meet to discuss their notes and so that I can guide them in their further exercises.

I see new advanced-level groups again after a week, then after two or three weeks. From then on, we decide the intervals together; on the average they are from three to five weeks. During group sessions we all practice the advanced-level exercises together; in individual instruction we simply discuss the results so far. Advanced-level work is particularly intensified when done in the form of retreats, or in the course of thematically related congresses. I once arranged a course so that for an hour every morning the group did advanced-level exercises together. The ten participants wrote their notes of their image-experiences privately in the afternoon, and most of them did a further session alone. At the next meeting we looked at these results and discussed them. Since one's involvement with AT never really stops, even now, from time to time, trainees from earlier years look me up and freshen up their AT, particularly the advanced level.

Demarcation lines

One is tempted to compare AT in general and the advanced level in particular with the many well-known relaxation and meditation techniques. Lengthy discussions of their differences tend to suffer from the sort of prejudice which exalts one's own method as the better one, or as the only true one. I have never been able to understand this attitude. In this book, I have been writing about AT, but this does not prevent my having a high opinion of other relaxation exercises or meditative techniques. My aim, as a psychotherapist, is to present the method under discussion as clearly as possible, and not to confuse it with others—especially not with those most similar to it.

There are two techniques I would like to mention in particular. One of them is ancient and known throughout the world: yoga. The other method has been developed in the past twenty years by Marianne Fuchs and has been regularly taught and demonstrated for about fifteen years at the Lindau Therapy Congress. It is called functional relaxation.

Yoga. With regard to yoga, two remarks must be made at the outset, because this Oriental method of meditation, linked with an influencing of the body, is as a method close to AT. Yoga developed in a cultural environment alien to most Europeans and Americans. This fact cannot be ignored. It is impossible here to present the sum of what yoga has to offer and to compare it with AT; since I myself do not practice yoga, I am not an authority on it. But, like most AT instructors, I am often asked what I think of yoga, or whether AT is not somewhat similar to it.

To these questions I always briefly reply somewhat as follows: These two methods, as far as their beneficial effects are concerned, are so similar that they cannot really compete with each other. Anyone who has learned yoga does not need AT. Those who have not learned it and who, in their own spiritual orientation, find Oriental attitudes totally alien, should, if they have the choice, learn AT and not yoga. Anyone who has already had some experience of yoga but who, for the sake of interest, would like to learn AT as well because at different adult-education establishments courses in both techniques are being offered, should decide at just whose table he wishes to dine. One must distinguish between wanting to obtain information about interesting techniques, and wanting to learn particular relaxation and meditation techniques in order to live with them. The latter motivation should be grounds enough for anyone, in the interest of his own economy of effort and the integration of his inner self, to decide for one or the other of the methods, and then to learn that one thoroughly and for keeps.

Functional relaxation. Under this general name, Marianne Fuchs has developed a technique which evolved from treatment of psychosomatically disturbed people, particularly from the treatment of asthma. She has also publicized this treatment under the name *"Atemrhythmisierende Entspannungstherapie"* ("relaxation therapy through rhythmic breathing"). The method of functional relaxation, in contrast to AT, works neither with set suggestive formulae nor with the goal of unfolding inner experiences in a state of trance. Functional relaxation is thus of great interest to the theory and practice of AT because—coming as it does to the same goal by a different means—it does not call the validity of AT in question and it can enrich it with important insights. Schultz himself knew Mrs. Fuchs personally and for many years took a sympathetically critical interest in her work. Both attempted to define the border areas between AT and functional relaxation and to exhaust the therapeutic possibilities of each method independently. According to my own knowledge of the method of functional relaxation, which I would describe as an experience of the body and the self (thus far much like AT) but without resorting to the induction and maintenance of a trance, this still largely unknown therapeutic method offers a most interesting counterpart to AT for further research and clinical practice.

CONCLUSION

I have attempted to present AT without writing a textbook, to give information about AT and the complexity of the method, and to describe it in such a way that the reader will wish to master it. As I have stressed many times, AT can be reliably learned only with the help of an instructor.

But this was not the only intention of the book. It is my hope that those who are already familiar with AT will read it as well, and will not only find much that they know already, but also discover new things to widen their horizons and deepen their insight.

Finally, this book is directed to those colleagues who teach AT and can compare their methods and experiences with those of the author. Seen from this point of view, it is a contribution to the discussion of questions of method and to the correlation of experiences.

I present a method here and communicate my personal experiences in order to make clear my own desire to reach a wider public after having established certain viable formulations in my talks with individual trainees and in the intimacy of small groups.

Anyone who writes about AT must be aware that he is contributing to the propagation and interpretation of a method whose founder is now world-famous. AT has survived many modifications, of which there has been no lack from the beginning. The great doctor J. H. Schultz, who developed in AT an easily mastered technique of self-composure, left his pupils with the memory of his own unshakable composure when confronted with various falsifications and simplifications of his method. His perseverance and inability to compromise were evident only when the basic principles of the method were being threatened to the detriment of the trainee. At present we are experiencing a broad popularization of AT which even includes unethical commercial exploitation. The ones who suffer from this are those interested but uninformed people who, on their own, cannot distinguish whether the many courses offered really are AT or some diluted relaxation technique that has no deeper effect. And thus there is reason enough to recall, as I have done here, the true basis of the AT method and its proper interpretation.

BIBLIOGRAPHY

It is beyond the scope of this book to list the wealth of scholarly contributions by the many authors who would deserve to be mentioned. The interested reader is here referred to the major works to which he can turn for further information.

Langen, D., *Der Weg des Autogenen Trainings,* Wissenschaftliche Buchgesellschaft, Darmstadt, 1968

Luthe, W., "Autogenic Training, Autogenes Training, Training Autogènee," in *Correlationes Psychosomaticae,* Grune & Stratton, New York/London 1964

Schultz, J. H. *Das Autogene Training. Konzentrative Selbstentspannung,* 13th edition, Thieme-Verlag, Stuttgart 1970 (Especially Part B—"Zur Theorie der Methode" p. 269 ff.)

Schultz, J. H., and W. Luthe, *Autogenic Methods,* Grune & Stratton, New York/London 1969 (Six volumes, especially the first volume, edited by Luthe, *"Autogenic Therapy"*)

Stokvis, B., and E. Wiesenhütter, *Der Mensch in der Entspannung. Lehrbuch autosuggestiver und übender Verfahren der Psychotherapie und Psychosomatik,* 3rd edition, Hippokrates, Stuttgart 1971

Thomas, K., *Praxis der Selbsthypnose des Autogenen Trainings* (after J. H. Schultz). Formelhafte Vorsatzbildung und Oberstufe, 2nd edition, Thieme-Verlag, Stuttgart 1972

Wallnöfer, H., *Seele ohne Angst. Hypnose, Autogenes Training, Entspannung,* 3rd edition, Hoffmann und Campe, Hamburg 1972

Wiesenhütter, E. (ed.) *Hypnose und Autogenes Training in der psychoso-matischen Medezin,* Stuttgart 1971. Schriftenreihe zur Theorie und Praxis der mediz. Psychologie, vol. 17. See particularly the article "Atemrhythmisierende Entspannungstherapie bei psychosomatischen Störungen" by Marianne Fuchs.